A PRAYER BEFORE DAWN

A Nightmare in Thailand

Billy Moore

First published by Maverick House in 2014
This paperback edition published by Maverick House in 2018

Copyright © 2014 Billy Moore

6 7 8 9 10

Maverick House,
Unit 33,
Stadium Business Park,
Ballycoolin,
Dublin 11, Ireland.
D11HY40
www.maverickhouse.com

info@maverickhouse.com

A CIP catalogue record for this book is available from the British Library.

ISBN 978-1-908518-63-7
ISBN 978-1-908518-53-8 (ebook)

The paper used in this book comes from wood pulp of managed forests. For every tree
felled, at least one tree is planted, thereby renewing natural resources.

Printed and bound in Great Britain by CPI Group (UK) Ltd, Croydon CR0 4YY

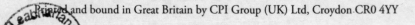

This book is dedicated to my mother,
a small woman with a big heart.

PROLOGUE

A YOUNG THAI, no older than twenty-five, ran past me, his face showing pure terror. He slowed and turned to look at his assailant, who then passed me swinging his metal chair, striking the victim's head. He lost balance, slipped, and hit the concrete with a loud thud. Another man appeared with a nine-inch knife, and stood over the young man's body.

A crowd gathered; even trusties stood and watched as the older man repeatedly plunged the knife into the young Thai's flesh. It wasn't done in frenzy; it was slow, cold, and calculated. Still no one helped or attempted to intervene. They all just stared, while a few shouted *teng kao* and *kaa man*.

I knew enough Thai to understand that the crowd was shouting "stab him" and "kill it". The knifeman kept thrusting the blade into the young man's body, each time sinking it in up to the handle. The knife went into his neck, lower back, chest, legs, and stomach; so many times I lost count.

I stood only a few feet away, watching in fascination and feeling guilty. Finally the victim lay still and quiet, in a pool of his own blood. It was horrible. I felt bad for not helping. But what could I do? This was a Thai problem. And I was a foreigner, one of many in Klong Prem prison.

More than a week passed before I could sleep without replaying the murder of the young man, over and over again in my head, in slow motion. This was the reality of life in Klong Prem, a place described by the prime minister of Thailand as a zoo to house the nation's most dangerous criminals. And little did I know that this was just the beginning of what was to be, for me, three years of a waking nightmare.

Chapters

1

Rocky Roads

STANDING ON A prison roof is a great way to get noticed. And that's what I wanted – to get noticed; to be acknowledged; for someone to look at me and see me for who I was, a small frightened child who was never allowed to grow up. I was desperate and full of fear. I couldn't live life on life's terms; this was my only escape. I needed help; I just didn't know how to ask for it. To me, being on the roof was the answer.

Sadly, for the time being no one was about to ask me to tell them my life story; all they wanted was to get me and my fourteen fellow inmates off the roof. HMP Liverpool was on lockdown and seventy feet below us a full complement of guards in riot gear were spread out and craning their necks to look up at us.

Discontent had been bubbling all day. It was one of the hottest days of the year. The whispers went around: "We're staying out, they can't make us go back into those sweatboxes." There was a buzz of excitement which mounted and spread from man to man like electricity. It was forbidden; it was a mutiny; we were going to defy the system.

At first they closed the gates, left us in the yard and watched us from behind barbed wire and seven-foot-high locked gates. They watched us the way people observe dangerous animals in the zoo. They said nothing.

There were about a hundred and fifty of us – the guards knew better than to try and take us on and aggravate an already explosive situation. They had all the time in the world. We took our shirts off and let the sun beat down on our pale prison skins. Big mistake! We wanted to get up on the roof – that was our objective and to get there we needed makeshift ropes. The word had spread quickly that something was going down in the exercise yard. Dinner time had come and gone without the usual queue of hungry inmates shuffling along, metal trays in hand.

"What's going on?" an inmate asked.

"What the hell's going on?" another shouted.

"A sit-in, in the yard," came the reply from another group of inmates.

"Where?"

"In the yard, man."

The screws were flapping around, yelling, trying to get the others back into their cells and away from the situation.

Back in their cells the guys wanted to be in on the action. If they couldn't get up onto the roof, at least they could help the men in the yard get there. Men started to pass sheets out of the cell windows. Brown sheets floated down into the yard and were tied together into ropes. All we needed was a climber. Actually what we needed was Spider-Man, and we had him!

His name was Austie, a cat burglar with a stutter. He was a local lad who was game to try anything. He tied the sheets around his waist and got up onto the shoulders of the tallest man available. From there he grabbed onto a drainpipe and, by getting his tiny feet into the smallest of crevices, he shimmied up the pipe. We watched breathless as Austie inched higher and higher. As we looked on, dirt and debris fell in our eyes and all around. He was getting there. Even the screws must have been impressed because, when Austie made it to the roof and stood with his hands in the air like Rocky Balboa, the whole prison erupted with shouts and whistles and yells of approval. That was Austie's finest hour, no doubt!

Three guys successfully made it up onto the roof, and then it was my turn. The last bit of climbing I remembered doing was when I was a ten-year-old and thieved eggs from birds' nests. I could hear one of the landing staff shout "no chance, fat arse!" and a chorus of sniggers from the other screws.

"Fat arse?" I'd show them. I scrambled up the sheets, helped by the men above who pulled me up as best they could.

At the top, hearing the jubilation, I felt like a superstar. But the thrill was short-lived. I was getting what I wanted for sure. I was being noticed. But not in the way I wanted. Suddenly, I felt alone and scared. I knew I'd have to come down sooner or later and for a split second I contemplated taking the quickest route. For that moment I envisaged myself splattered all over the yard, my blood drying fast in the scorching heat, the detested screws having to scrub away at the bits of me which would be plastered all over the walls and tarmac.

But that's not the kind of person I am.

In fact, I was brought down sixteen hours later in a cherry-picker, suffering from sunstroke. I spent a night in the hospital wing and then the next seven months in solitary confinement. I got a few kicks and a few punches from the guards – nothing I wasn't already used to. It was a bit of an anti-climax, really.

So much for my big cry for help.

It was much later on in my life that I learned the kind of really bad things that can happen to you in prison.

I was thirty years old when this happened but I'd been in and out of jail since I was seventeen: dangerous driving, burglary, robbery, violence, drugs.

Drugs, of course. That's where it all started. I was smoking weed with my mates from the age of sixteen. I graduated to smoking smack a year later and my world changed.

Smack made me vomit at first but that feeling of being wrapped in cotton wool, protected and secure, was worth the discomfort. I couldn't get enough of it. As you may have guessed, security, protection and love were things sadly missing from my life. You've probably heard it all before, the alcoholic, violent dad, the valiant mother brutalised and broken down by caring for six children and having to deal with a violent husband. The endless poverty, the 70s council estates rigidly divided into ganglands, the Toxteth riots in the 80s.

I could paint an endless, dreary picture of my childhood but one memory sums it up.

It was my birthday. I was 12 years old. My mum had been saving for weeks to buy me some new clothes from a catalogue. I'd chosen them myself: silver-grey cords and a silver-grey patterned top. Smart. I wore them with pride all day. It was my birthday – no one else's day, just mine. Not Father's Day or Mother's Day or Christmas Day or any other day. My day, my birthday. And I thought to myself, you know what? I'm 12 today and I can stay out until half past seven with my mates instead of being home by seven. And that's what I did. When I got home I expected my five younger siblings to be there to sing me Happy Birthday; expected my mum to have a cake baked.

I was stopped in my tracks by my dad.

My father, Tony: fifteen stone, five-ten, an ex-boxer and a heavy drinker. He was habitually unemployed, a social scrounger, a bad husband, and a violent father.

"Where the hell have you been? What time do you call this?"

I told him: "It's my birthday."

"Come here and I'll give you a damn birthday present, you ginger-headed bastard."

Perhaps I should have run, but I froze instead, and the next thing I knew, his fist had landed squarely on my nose and blood was spurting all over my silver-grey top and my silver-grey trousers.

My mum was screaming: "You evil bastard, leave him alone."

My brothers and sisters sat at the jelly-laden table, eyes staring, chins wobbling, tears filling their eyes, paper party hats on their heads. My mum started to tear the clothes off me. "They'll stain," she kept repeating. I stood there half-naked, shivering in the kitchen while my dad shambled off into the living room to watch TV. It wasn't the first time I'd been beaten and it wasn't the last. And I later discovered that heroin was a refuge, a warm happy place to curl up in where no one could get to me, where I could have a real birthday whenever I wanted.

No fear. No pain. Perfect.

2

Rehab

IT HAD BEEN a long and uncomfortable journey from the prison. I was escorted to the drug rehabilitation centre by Paul, a probation officer, a good man who wanted to see me recover from my drug addiction.

We arrived at the rehab centre, a beautiful mock-Tudor mansion in Somerset. The house itself was surrounded by beautiful green hills. It was summer, the smell of freshly-cut grass was in the air, and I could see a lily pond and hear frogs croaking. The scenery was amazing. I got out of the car, stretching, and looked up at the clear, blue summer sky. I took a deep breath. I was free. No more long, lonely hours in solitary confinement. It was time for Paul to leave. We said our goodbyes and he wished me good luck.

I made my way to the main entrance, not sure what to expect once inside, but I knew I wanted to stop taking drugs. However, my idea of being drug-free was to stop using class A drugs – the killers, heroin and crack cocaine. They were my problem, not the softer drugs like alcohol, cannabis and pharmaceuticals. I could control my use of them, couldn't I?

A group of what I can only describe as junkies welcomed me at the main reception. One guy in particular headed towards me, a rough-looking character with a couple of front teeth missing and a huge smile on his face. He had his hands held out wide, and in a cockney accent said, "Awight, bruv! I'm René." Instead of shaking my hand he attempted to give me a hug.

"Back off, you faggot!" I said through clenched teeth. "Don't touch me."

"Sweet bruv, it's OK. It's what we do here. Just showing a bit of love," he said defensively.

"I don't want any faggot love," I growled. Love didn't exist in my world.

Walking away from the group I sat down in one of the cheap plastic chairs in the waiting room. A small balding guy wearing glasses came over to where I was seated, and introduced himself as Mark. He told me he would be my counsellor. He took me up some stairs and showed me into a huge room which had three single beds inside. Nobody else would be sharing the room with me, but Mark told me that could change.

He left me to settle in. I moved over to a bed, laid back on it and closed my eyes. Tired and exhausted, I fell quickly asleep.

The following day, Mark called me to his office for a one-to-one counselling session. He just sat there with a thoughtful look on his face. I began to feel uncomfortable. He held eye contact, and then started firing questions at me. Why was I here? What did I expect from the treatment?

I answered. He asked me how I was feeling. This confused me because I didn't know how I felt. He waited patiently for me to answer.

"OK, I guess," I responded.

"OK is not a feeling," he said.

"I'm fine," I said, more confidently.

"We don't do fine. FUCKED UP, INSECURE, NEUROTIC and EMOTIONAL," he rattled off. "I want a feeling from you, William!"

This guy's really nuts, I thought to myself, trying to control my rage.

"OK, how about horny? That's a feeling, right?" I asked Mark.

"Yes, that's a feeling."

"OK: I so horny. Love you long time." I was remembering a line from the movie Full Metal Jacket and laughing at my own humour. Mark wasn't amused and asked me if I thought this was all a game, and didn't I want to recover? Of course I wanted to recover. I just didn't understand what my feelings had to do with me using drugs.

I was soon going to find out.

I left Mark's office and bumped into René, the hugger.

"All right, bruv, no hard feelings hey?"

I ignored him. I wasn't here to make friends. I was a loner and felt comfortable that way.

"Group therapy is this way, bruv," said René, pointing to a huge oak door at the far end of the corridor. "You're in my group. It's paramount you attend. Rules, you understand."

I reluctantly followed René to the main hall. It was massive inside, with high ceilings, and an old chandelier hanging up in the centre of the room. The windows were long and wide, and a bright light shone through the dirty coloured net curtains. The room smelled old and musty so I opened one of the windows to let in some fresh air. There were eight chairs in the centre of the room, placed in a circular formation. We seemed to be the only ones there.

"Group's at 9.15, bruv," drawled René, the hugger.

I had fifteen minutes to kill before the group session started. The chairs were comfy. I closed my eyes and waited. A bell sounded that signalled everyone to the group. Soon people started wandering into the room and filling the seats. I opened my eyes to see who my groupies were.

Opposite me was a heavily pregnant woman, young with beautiful long blonde hair that seemed to shine in the sunlight. She had a pretty face with a spat of golden brown freckles on both cheeks. "Hi, my name's Suzanne," she said, introducing herself. Her accent was from the West Midlands somewhere. I smiled back and nodded. More people entered and took up the rest of the seats.

Dave Mac introduced himself as one of the head counsellors; he looked like a flash bastard with his designer clothes and his goatee. He had previously been an addict, but had been clean for fifteen years. He was in his forties but aimed to look younger, with his young ghetto clothes.

I was new to the group. Dave asked me to share a little about myself; this was normal, he assured me.

I told myself I looked better than the rest of the group. I had spent a couple of years in prison, hitting the gym hard and eating porridge. I didn't look like your typical junkie, so I lied. I told the other members of the group I was here because I snorted a bit too much cocaine. It sounded better than saying I was a smackhead or a dirty, flea-bitten crack-fiend.

"So you're just a sniffer then, pal?" a Scottish guy asked me. "By the way, my name's Alex. I'm an alcoholic."

Dave asked me if taking cocaine was my only problem. "Yeah," I answered, not believing my own lie. He continued to drill me, asking questions such as whether I could control my drug use, and would I be prepared to live a drug-free life.

It was impossible to imagine, I told him. I suppose just smoking cannabis would be OK.

"Wrong!" he said. For me to live a normal life and become a productive member of society, I would have to stop. Everything had to stop.

I thought maybe he was over-reacting, so I played the game and went along with what he said.

I could see René looking at me with an intent expression on his face.

"What are you looking at, poof?" I said.

"I ain't no poof, bruv! What's your problem?"

Dave asked me why I called René a poof, so I told him about the hugging stuff and how he wanted to feel me up. Everybody laughed, making me feel angry.

"How long have you been here now? One, two days? René is not a poof, gay or homosexual."

"So would you let me give you a hug, Billy?" said Suzanne.

"Well, yeah."

"Would a hug suggest I wanted to have sex with you?"

"I'm not sure, would you?" I said, hoping yes would be the answer.

"We just want to show you that we care," said René.

"What are you afraid of?" asked Dave.

I was afraid of being honest – showing people the real me. I avoided feelings, I came from a place where you didn't show or express how you felt. Only the weak were vulnerable. I didn't feel comfortable about being confronted with such personal questions.

"What do you fear?"

"Nothing!" I told Dave. "Can we move on? I'm getting bored."

Dave addressed the group, wanting a feelings check before we left.

"How do you feel, Alex?"

"I feel angry."

Suzanne was feeling fat but content. René was relieved. Other members of the group gave different feelings.

"OK, Billy, how do you feel?"

"I feel OK."

Everybody said in unison, "WE DON'T DO OK!"

What did they want to hear? Crazy nut jobs! That I was scared? That I wanted to scream? To cry? Show people I was human? That I was hiding behind a mask. These were feelings I couldn't express.

"We need a feeling," Dave said.

"To hell with you and your feelings, Dave!"

"You're feeling angry, pal!" said Alex.

This was true. I could see therapy was going to be tough. Dave called an end to the session. I left the room and went for a smoke to help me calm down.

During the day, when there was no group or counselling session going on, I would wander the grounds of the treatment centre and spend hours looking at the amazing scenery. I had never been to the countryside before. I couldn't even recall a time where I had left my own city, except maybe once as a child, when my parents had taken us all to a Butlin's holiday camp in Wales. It was so long ago I couldn't even remember what the place was like.

I sat on a bench and lit up a cigarette. I'd had enough of smoking but like everything else I thought it was impossible to stop. Maybe I never would.

"Hello, have you got a fag?" It was one of the female residents, a small plain-looking girl in her early thirties, I guessed. I passed her one and gave her a light. She smiled, thanked me and sat down on the bench. She told me her name was Tracy. She had been there almost three months and now, with only a couple of weeks left, was a trusted member of the house.

"I get to go to the beach in Weston-super-Mare tomorrow," she said excitedly.

"Fantastic," I replied sarcastically. However, she was so wrapped up in her own thoughts that she didn't seem to notice.

"We get to go shopping. I can buy you something if you want, maybe a stick of rock or some candy. Would you like that?"

"Hmm, how about you buy me a bottle of brandy instead?"

"Oh no! It's not allowed. You could get dismissed!"

"Not if no one knows. We could drink it together by the lily pond. What do you say?" I could see she was thinking about it. I smiled and gave her a knowing wink, the sort that said maybe we could have more than just a drink.

"What, just you and me? And no one will know?"

"Of course, mum's the word."

"OK. Meet me at the lily pond tomorrow at 7.00pm. I'll bring the brandy."

"Don't worry, I'll be there," I said quietly at her retreating back.

The following day dragged. I had my doubts about Tracy buying the alcohol. Maybe she would get scared or, even worse, grass me up. I knew others were using drugs in the rehab centre, so I wasn't alone.

I made my way down to the lily pond just before 7.00pm and waited on one of the benches, chain smoking while looking at the huge green lilies floating on the water. It was a quiet evening, serene in fact. I was lost in the beauty of it all. The drab, grey prison walls were a distant memory. Life was different out here, much calmer. I felt warm hands cover my eyes.

"Guess who?"

"Jennifer Lopez," I said, knowing quite well she was no J.Lo; more like Miss Methadone 2004.

"No! It's me, silly. Tracy."

"Did you get the brandy?" I asked nervously.

"Yes, of course," she beamed.

She pulled it out of her bag. I took it from her, opened the bottle and had a huge swig, then passed the bottle back to Tracy. She was rubbing my leg and smiling at me.

"Did I do good, Billy?"

"Yeah you did good," I said, leaning down to kiss her on the lips. She responded by rubbing her hand over my crotch, arousing me. I wanted sex, not love; quick meaningless sex. No conversations. I wanted to use Tracy.

It was over in minutes. I quickly pulled up my jeans, finished off the brandy and left Tracy to sort herself out. She was accustomed to being used. She was like everyone else I came across.

Later, I found myself knocking on Neil's door. Like me, he was struggling to give up drugs entirely. He had a small stash of cannabis which we smoked. He also had Mogadon sleeping pills. He was tall, tanned and skinny and had been sent to the rehab by his mother to get off heroin. He smuggled the drugs in to help with his withdrawal.

"I can't do it without the sleepers; the sleepless nights kill me, Bill."

I had done my cold turkey in a prison cell. The sweats, the shits, the agonizing cramps. I had been through it all. It was easy to forget the pain and misery once it was over. You would tell yourself it hadn't been that bad.

I felt sorry for Neil; he was only twenty-two. He gave me a handful of pills which I dry-swallowed, grabbed the offered splif and toked away. It had been a while since I had last used drugs, but now I wanted more. I wanted heroin. I was obsessed, and the room started spinning – the drink mixed with the cocktail of drugs was taking effect. My mind went blank.

The next morning, I woke up at the bottom of the stairs, close to the main reception area. The day after my drink and drug spree, my head was banging and my mouth felt like an old flip-flop.

"Are you OK, pal? It looks like you've pissed your trousers." It was Scottish Alex.

A few residents were staring at me, shaking their heads. René stepped forward and looked down at me.

"Come on and give me your hand, bruv," René offered.

I grabbed his outstretched hand and pulled myself up. I walked quickly back up the stairs to my room.

"Surrender! It's your only chance," shouted René at my retreating back.

Once I had cleaned myself up, I was summoned to Dave's office. He had heard what had happened.

"Billy, do you want to be here?"

"Yeah, Dave."

"You broke the rules; you're going to have to leave."

Fear gripped me. Leave! Go where? I knew I was going to end up either dead or in prison. I make it a rule not to beg but I did that day. I pleaded with Dave to give me a chance, promising him the world, and at that moment I meant it. I really wanted to be drug-free. That prison cell was now a fresh memory.

Dave turned and spoke quietly to a female member of staff. He finally returned his attention to me and said: "OK, one more chance."

"Thank you! I won't let you down."

"Don't let yourself down. It's about you now."

Relief swept over me. A change happened to me that day. I was determined to fight this – I pulled out my cigarettes and vowed that they were going in the bin. You're not clean until you give up the nicotine, I told myself.

To keep myself busy and my mind occupied during my free time I would punch the living daylights out of the heavy bag Dave Mac had brought in for people who wanted to release some anger or pent-up aggression. This kept me busy as well as fit.

One weekend, after spending four months inside the treatment centre, I was allowed a three-day home leave. This was it, the test. How would I deal with the real world and reality?

I was lucky I had built up a network of friends during the time I was in treatment, and one of these friends took me to Manchester during my three days at home to meet Ricky Hatton, the WBA light welterweight boxing champion. Ricky was in training for his fight against Kostya Tszyu, a national hero in his adopted Australia. My mum loves Ricky Hatton; she said his demeanour and behaviour reminded her of me, and that we even resembled each other.

This was a taste of what being clean had in store for me, meeting wonderful people like Ricky who did amazing work for charity. He even posed for pictures and signed a pair of boxing gloves for me. I enjoyed the three days away from treatment, and being amongst my family and drug-free was an amazing sensation. It was the greatest feeling, and one that was coming back.

Over the coming months, my life changed. I had fought in the ring, on the streets and on prison landings. I thought I was tough, until I went to war with my own feelings. I completed the primary treatment care and joined René in the second stage of my recovery.

We became friends. A new chapter in my life was about to begin.

3

Thailand

I AM A world-class, card-carrying pleasure seeker.

This was my first thought as I stepped off the plane at Bangkok's Don Muang international airport. The heat was incredible; it was so hot and yet it was November. Twelve hours earlier, back in the UK, the weather had been freezing and miserable, and now, here I was in a tropical country with three months of sun and fun ahead of me. Thailand is where you will find some of the most mouth-watering delights on the face of this planet, spiced with garlic, ginger, lemon-grass, basil and chillies.

"Welcome to amazing Thighland," whooped Joey excitedly. "The land of no tits and sloppy shits," he said, slapping me on the back. Joey and I had been friends for almost a year now, ever since I had completed rehab. He invited me on what he called a trip of a lifetime and was bursting with energy.

"Billy, if you're afraid of dying, it shows you have a life worth keeping," he once said to me when I was in the early days of recovery.

He had visited Thailand the year before and was now an expert on the country and its culture. He regretted having taken his girlfriend on that first trip. Alone this time, and without a partner to cramp his style, he'd be free to enjoy all that Thailand had to offer. He was in his element.

"Drink bottled water. Always wear a condom. Be careful of men with tits and lipstick!" he said, rolling off a list of do's and don'ts.

Once we were through customs, we took a taxi to Khao San Road, one of Bangkok's major tourist areas, which was bustling with activity and traders of every description. You could purchase anything here from forged documents to herbal flip-flops. There were loud shouts in broken English – of cheap rooms, cheap women, cheap copies; the whole city seemed to be touting its wares.

"Hello. Greetings, great sirs, you are wanting cheap suit? Very good quality by Mr Giorgio himself," lied the Indian trader who followed us half-way up Khao San.

"Piss off, Elvis, we don't need an ugly suit in weather like this," Joey said, dismissing him with a wave of his hand.

"Leave him alone, lad. He's just grafting, trying to pay the bills, the same as us," I said, throwing the guy a few baht.

I was excited we had decided to come to Thailand. Joey promised to show me what I had been missing all my life, and I suppose that was living. I remember my counsellor once told me that if I stayed drug-free my life would improve, and he wasn't wrong. The awful memories of my father – drunk, out of work, sleeping on park benches, the beatings he inflicted on my mother and me and the rest of his children – these were a thing of the past as he had left our life. I had my family back and good friends who were there to help and support me if I needed it. I'd quit smoking, I trained in the gym regularly and even ate more healthily. On the whole, life was good and I intended to enjoy it.

We found the only non-cockroach-infested guest house in Bangkok that came within our budget – cheap enough but with air con that didn't work. The room had two single beds, each wrapped in dirty-coloured cream sheets with no pillows.

"No Sucking in Bed," the sign said above one of the single beds. "Joey, you're out of luck, there's no sucking in bed," I said, laughing at the translation mistake that should have said "No Smoking in bed".

We met a couple of guys from England downstairs at the bar – Jay and his nephew Charlie. Jay had spent a lot of time in Thailand and could speak the language. He was willing to show us around Bangkok's red-light entertainment districts – Patpong, Soi Cowboy and Nana Plaza – which he described as heaving with go-go bars, strip bars and sex shows.

"You have to see the shows while you're here," suggested Jay.

"What kind of shows?" I asked, confused, but also curious to find out what the Bangkok nightlife had to offer.

He told me about shows I never would have imagined, and couldn't wait to see.

Nana Plaza was full of neon lights, loud music and cheap booze. The place looked like it belonged on the set of Blade Runner, wires hanging down, sparks flashing, the dirty smoke from the exhausts of tuk tuks (three-wheeled motorcycles) making the air impossible to breathe and your clothes filthy black.

We followed Jay to a go-go bar. Inside it was dark. There was a stage in the centre on which a lot of beautiful but bored-looking girls danced around poles. We took our seats. Joey and I didn't drink so we ordered water which earned us a cheap look from the young girl who served us. Jay and Charlie each had a Singha beer and received a warm smile.

Jay called over a couple of girls wearing skimpy bikinis and spoke to them in Thai. One of them sat on his lap, leaving the other one to squeeze in between Joey and me.

"Feel how smooth their skin is; it feels like silk," said Jay, stroking the girl's naked stomach. Joey's eyes were wide with lust. I watched as he glided his hand over the girl who sat between us, stroking her leg and smelling her hair. I looked at Jay who smiled and gave me a mischievous wink. Something was wrong with these women. I took a closer look at the girl Joey was fondling. Although it was dark and smoky in the club, I could see what appeared to be a small lump on her throat.

SHIT! It was a man, one of those "she things" Joey had warned me about before we came here.

Jay raised a finger to his lips. "Shush," he said quietly and winked. But this had to be one of those ladyboys. You could hardly tell it was a man. He had beautiful, long, black flowing hair and a sexy body.

Shit, it was scary.

Joey was up on the dance floor, squeezing the ladyboy's bum and nuzzling his/her neck. Jay was laughing out loud and the tears streamed down his face at the sight of Joey staring deep into the ladyboy's eyes. Love was written all over his face, yet Joey was unaware that the she was a he.

I wasn't going to tell him, what with him being an expert on Thailand. I laughed with Jay: serves him right!

Joey asked me not to breathe a word of what happened in Nana Plaza that night.

"But you kissed a man!" I said, feigning disgust.

"Come on, Billy, I didn't know. You've got to admit though, he was a good-looking fella," he said in his defence.

"You had your tongue down his throat. And you took his phone number," I said, shaking my head then pretending to be sick.

"Yeah, well, let's just forget that for now. He told me his name was Bob. Can you believe that? Bob," he said. "He could have chosen a better name than that, like Sylvia or something womanly."

"Never mind. What happens on holiday stays on holiday," I said, saving him further embarrassment.

We travelled to various parts of Thailand, Pattaya being one of them. Pattaya is a seedy sex resort where Joey felt most at home. I soon learned that his primary purpose in Thailand was sex, not the country or its culture as he had told me. He didn't want to visit temples or the country's other amazing sights. He was more comfortable in brothels. This caused problems as I wanted to soak up Thailand's culture and warm, friendly atmosphere, so we parted company after only a couple of weeks' travelling.

Just before I left England to explore this far distant land, one day I was enjoying coffee in Bristol with a close friend of mine, Krissie.

"Billy, what are you running away from?" she asked, knowing how hard I had worked (washing cars, scrubbing dishes, babysitting, cleaning windows and providing cheap labour) to save what little money I had for my trip. I would take on any job, I had objectives and I intended to achieve the goals I had set for myself.

I sat back, coffee in hand, and stared back at Krissie, who was around the same age as me and from North London. She was a pretty girl with big, brown eyes and a warm smile.

"Who says I'm running away? Maybe I'm running towards where I want to be," I coolly told her.

I wanted to find out what I liked about life and what I wanted out of it. Who did I like? What did life have in store for me? Drugs, prison and near death was the old life I had lived; now it was a new me and I needed to discover a whole new way of living, without the dependency on drugs or the worry of a mother praying that we don't die today and that the front door won't be kicked in by the police. I was sure there was something out there in Thailand that would make me feel alive for the first time in my life.

It was a long journey north from Bangkok. The train took twelve hours to reach Chiang Mai.

Once I got there, I would have left the place sooner if it hadn't been for the attentions of Nina, a beautiful Japanese-American woman.

Nina had lived in Chiang Mai for eight years. She was a bored housewife married to an American businessman old enough to be her father, whose work took him away from home for long periods of time, leaving the lovely Nina alone. She just wanted a bit of fun – the no-strings type.

Nina had a dog named Lily, a small, black French poodle that she took everywhere in a wooden basket. I hated that dog. For a start, it was a sex addict and wouldn't leave my leg alone. But Lily was also a jealous dog with issues. It stayed with its mistress 24/7, even in bed, which made having sex with her something of a mission.

Nina was easily impressed and I would fill her head full of magic, spinning tales of how I was the greatest boxer since Cassius Clay. Between the ages of thirteen and sixteen, in the late 80s, I boxed for England schoolboys. I had fought in Ireland and across England, winning eleven out of my fourteen fights. My trainer, John, had high hopes for me before I allowed the drugs to steal away a promising boxing career.

Nina and I went to watch a Muay Thai kick-boxing show on Loi Kroi Road, close to the local night bazaar. This was Nina's first time at a boxing venue.

"Hey, Billy, why don't you fight one of these guys? I want to see you kick ass," she squealed with excitement.

I just wanted to enjoy the show, not take part in it. However, I heard myself say, "OK." I reasoned it couldn't be any different from the kind of boxing I was used to.

The last time I had fought was six months earlier. I had left the rehab in Somerset not yet free enough to trust myself to be too far away from the centre. I had moved to Bristol and there fought against a doorman, a guy from Jordan. We had met in a sauna at the gym I trained at and he asked me if I liked to fight, whether I would fight him. Although I thought it was a strange proposition to put to me in a sauna, my pride would not allow me to say no and I agreed immediately. We met the next day in the car park. The fight lasted a minute.

I had beaten the living daylights out of the Jordanian bouncer so I felt confident of my chances here in Thailand against one of these skinny wombats.

I made my way over to the ring and approached a group of young Thai men who were obviously fighters. They smiled but eyed me suspiciously while smoking and drinking their whiskey.

"I wanna fight," I said, while miming boxing to emphasize my meaning. A small Thai guy covered in home-made tattoos and wearing blue boxing shorts came towards me.

"I fight you 200 baht, OK?" he said, with a huge smile spread across his battered face.

"OK, where's the shorts?" I said, handing him the money. He walked over to an old couple and split the money with them.

I changed for the fight and kissed Nina on the lips. In her high-pitched American accent she screamed, "You go, honey, you beat his ass."

No problem, I thought. He's small, he drinks and smokes. This should be over in minutes. It'll be a good way to impress the lovely Nina.

Ding! Ding! The bell sounded for the first round.

BANG! I was kicked in the face. I wasn't expecting that. Then again, this time in the lower limbs. Pain shot through my leg. I threw a flurry of punches, missing my opponent and hitting only air. This little fella was in and out fast.

The round ended without me laying a glove on him. Nina was in my corner and splashed water over my face, while "Jackie Chan" in the opposite corner had an entourage of fellow-boxers pouring whiskey down his throat.

"What's wrong, honey," Nina asked, concern deep in her voice.

"Nothing! I'm just warming up," I lied.

"OK, go beat him, baby. Beat his little ass," she said as she pulled away the stool.

Ding! Ding! Round two.

This time I went out quickly and trapped him in the corner, smashing my fists into his head. He went down but bounced back up fast, then charged at me and took hold of my neck. His knees were ripping into my ribs. Pain seared through my body. I pushed him away and caught him with a right hand. He went down and I could see from the starry expression in his eyes that he was close to losing consciousness. Screams came from his corner – his friends were egging him on: "*Nimdam, farang jeb.*" They were telling him that I was hurt. The encouragement spurred him on and his next attack was ferocious.

"I love you, baby. Kick his dumb ass," roared Nina over the loud Thai music that was pumping out through the speakers.

My pride took over. I had to see this through. There was one more round. This was difficult; we were both hurt but continued to pound each other, neither of us prepared to give up. His knees kept attacking my ribs while my punches were smashing into his bloody face. This small fighting machine was tough.

The bell sounded. The fight was finally over.

I limped away from the ring holding my ribs. Nina hugged me, causing me to wince. "You're the best, honey. I love you," she cooed. Well, at least I had impressed someone, I thought.

"Hey, *farang*, you OK?" shouted Nimdam while showing me the universal thumbs-up sign. I managed a smile that felt more like a grimace as I walked away.

Somehow I knew I would be coming back.

4

Muay Thai

PROBABLY THE MOST famous Muay Thai kick-boxer of all time was Nai Khanom Tom. He was one of 30,000 Thais taken prisoner by the Burmese in 1767 during an attack on Ayudhya – then the capital of Siam. At a large Buddhist festival held in Yangon (Rangoon) the following year, the Siamese pugilist was invited to represent his fellow prisoners of war in a round of public boxing matches. Before a crowd of hundreds, Khanom Tom unleashed a barrage of bare fists, feet, knees and elbows, and defeated ten Burmese fighters in succession (some say it was a dozen), earning the respect of the royal court and winning his freedom. He returned to Siam a national hero.

After Khanom Tom's famous bouts, a member of the Burmese royal court is said to have remarked, "Every part of the Thai is blessed with venom. Even with his bare hands, he can fell nine or ten opponents!"

Many of Thailand's national archives, including the Chupphasaht, a detailed Thai martial arts manual, were destroyed during a mid-eighteenth century Burmese invasion. The earliest known Thai written reference, found in chronicles written in Chiang Mai during the earlier Lana era (1296-1558 38AD), mentions a ferocious style of unarmed combat that decided the fate of the Thai kings. During these early days, combatants' hands were wrapped in thick horsehide for maximum impact and minimum knuckle damage. In grudge matches, the hands were bound with glue-soaked cotton or hemp and then dipped in ground glass to inflict maximum injury and pain.

Thais are true warriors and on one famous occasion in the 1970s, Hong Kong's top five kung fu masters travelled to Thailand to compete against Thai boxers. The Chinese were all knocked out in less than six and a half minutes, earning Muay Thai the right to be called the most devastating martial art in the world.

Months passed by and I was alone again. Nina had gone back to her husband. There was nothing back in England for me but painful memories, lonely nights and cold weather, so I decided to stay on in Thailand.

I came back to the Muay Thai boxing camp wanting to learn, appreciate and endure this ancient art of fighting. I was introduced to Mama and Papa who were and still are the owners of the gym. The pair were then quite old, their skin wrinkled from a lifetime of exposure to a sweltering sun. Their boxers put on staged fights and collected tips that would help them support their families. I was short on money so couldn't afford the extortionate prices that other Muay Thai schools charged.

Mama and Papa were a kind couple but, like many Thais, they were greedy, devious and cunning by nature. They agreed to allow the other boxers to mentor me in the art of Muay Thai, and in return I would use my English language skills to help the fighters by collecting tips from the tourists. I was the only foreigner crazy enough to be in this dusty, run-down gym. But I knew I belonged in the ring; it was the only place I felt alive and where mentally I was never hurt. It was out there in the real world that the pain was, the emotional stuff that always hurt me.

Every night I would get into the ring and put on staged shows with the other boxers. It was a fast way to learn. The guys showed me how to perform and execute all kinds of moves from defence to attack using my knees, elbows and feet. My existing boxing skills enabled me to learn pretty quickly and I was soon show-fighting regularly with the other boxers for tips which paid my bills. To fight like a Thai, I had to learn to live like a Thai and survive on these tips. I lived comfortably because the cost of living in Chiang Mai was low. It was cheaper to eat out than to cook in my apartment – and going out allowed me to experience more of the excitement of this culture that I craved.

The boxing arena in Loi Kroi Road was surrounded by girlie bars, thick with cigarette smoke, and visited by many tourists during the peak season, which is around November through until February. It was now mid-December so most nights we would collect good tips. This pleased Mama and Papa, who would usually give me a small share of the money they collected.

I spent most of my time at the arena. I trained hard and was at my physical peak. I'm built like a pit bull terrier, with incredible hand speed and more power than most Thai boxers. When sparring, I had to make more of an effort to catch my prey, but this kept me fit. Nimdam and his friend Yut, a small guy with most of his front teeth missing, would lounge around the gym, sharing cigarettes and drinking Sangsom whiskey from the 7-Eleven store.

"Farang, why you no drink?" Yut wanted to know.

"He cheap Charlie, number one," Nimdam teased.

How could I explain to them that if I started drinking again, I'd be on the same old journey? The same obsessions with the demons of alcohol and drug abuse would overwhelm me, and I would revert back to a life of crime and violence, wreaking havoc upon everybody around me again.

"Yeah, cheap Charlie, number one," I said, smiling back at them both.

Money motivates most people, especially Thais. They constantly talked about money, argued about money and, I imagined, dreamt about money. For Mama and Papa, their whole being revolved around making money. It totally dominated their lives. Show boxing just wasn't enough to pay the bills. The audience wanted real fights. So, each Monday night was "Fight Night". Papa would promote eleven championship bouts to a crowd of at least four hundred people.

These fights would have me sitting on the edge of my seat. Watching the superb technique of the fighters going to war amazed me. I wanted to be in that ring. I felt ready. I had been boxing for tips and green curries for over a year, and had beaten all of the eight show boxers in the camp. Even Nimdam would scream "Billy, bao bao krap" (go easy) every time we fought.

I hated the staged fights in which I was always made the winner to please the punters. I felt like a fraud. It was time for the real deal.

One day I plucked up courage and asked Papa to let me fight in one of the real shows. I told him I would split the money I earned with him if he allowed me to fight. No doubt influenced by the offer of money, he agreed to let me compete in one of the Monday night fights.

He set up a match between me and a guy named Kemphla, from a gym in Lampang, a small city just outside Chiang Mai. The fight was due to take place in two weeks, during which time I was to carry on fighting in the show bouts.

This is what I wanted, to battle with a seasoned boxer of equal size and weight, but not necessarily with the same skills that I possessed. It would be a real, hard-fought contest, an opportunity for me to prove myself as a proper Muay Thai fighter.

On the day of the fight I was alone in my room. As I lay on my bed and stared up at the huge propeller fan spinning above my head, I mentally prepared myself for what lay ahead that evening.

OK, what do I need to avoid? The holds? The knees? The elbows? I just needed to avoid him altogether. I was feeling nervous the whole day and fought the fight a million times in my head, playing and replaying every move I had been taught.

I arrived at the arena early. My fight was last on the card. Nimdam and Yut helped me to get ready, and rubbed boxing liniment all over my body. I only wished it was Kevlar, because it was surely only body armour that could protect me from a possible beating.

They were talking to me all the while, but I wasn't listening. I was watching the only other foreigner besides me who was fighting that night. He was a man called Johnson, from the Isle of Man, and entered the ring at number seven on the bill. I watched as this man got systematically destroyed within two rounds. He had been caught with a powerful forward elbow above his right eye, which knocked him out cold, his blood splattering the canvas.

Nimdam and Yut both looked at me. I could see concern etched on both of their young faces.

"Billy, you number one," Yut whispered in my left ear.

"Jai yen yen," (have a cool heart) said Nimdam, while squeezing my neck.

Mama came over to me with one of the flyers advertising the fights that night.

"Kor tort, Kuhn Billy," (sorry, Mr. Billy) she said, handing me the flyer. I could see my name next to a picture of a Chinese man, and my country of origin was given as Sweden. I laughed out loud. Now I was Chinese Billy from Sweden! Number eleven on the bill – cheap Charlie!

My name was called, and I entered the ring to the hypnotic beat of the traditional Muay Thai music. I eyed my opponent Kemphla from across the ring and watched as he performed the "ram muay," a ritual dance. He stretched and swayed as he paid his respects to spirits unseen. I was totally focused and ready for combat against this Thai master. The smoke-filled arena was filled to capacity.

The bell sounded. It was time! Kemphla came out strongly; he struck the back of my leg with a powerful round-house kick. He repeated the same kick only to have it blocked by my shin. Agony! My right leg went numb from the bone-on-bone impact.

We circled each other, both searching for weaknesses; we were like two lions trapped in a cage. When he attacked, the crowd were up on their feet and screaming. He teeped me (front kick), forcing me into a corner. His knees and elbows rained down on me ferociously, forcing me to defend myself. All I could do was cover up for protection.

The bell sounded, ending the first round. Papa was waiting for me in the corner, shadow boxing.

"OK, good!" Papa shouted above the roar of the excited crowd, who were baying for my blood.

Nimdam removed my gumshield and squirted water in my mouth and over my head and body to cool me down, while Yut rubbed frantically at my now red and bruising legs.

The bell sounded for the second round.

"Now fight. Box, farang, box!" roared Papa.

I charged out and switched from Muay Thai to boxing. I jabbed fast, connecting with my opponent's face, and stepped back when he attacked with a solid kick. Quickly I moved back in and, seeing an opening, smashed a right cross, square on his chin, knocking him off his feet. He hit the canvas hard. The crowd were standing again and screaming. Their allegiance was changing as they sensed my victory over their fallen hero.

Kemphla stayed down. He was hurt but conscious. I got down on my knees, held my hands together and waied (bowed) to show my respect for a great fighter.

"Geng mahk," (very good) he said, obviously impressed with my boxing skills.

It was over. I had won.

Papa and the other fighters from my camp were pleased and were all cheering and celebrating my first victory as a Muay Thai combatant. Both Nimdam and Yut hugged me tightly.

"Billy, good, very good," said Mama. As she kissed me on the forehead, I felt myself become a part of the camp at last.

At that moment, I knew this is where I belonged – in an old, battered, run-down gym with a blood-splattered canvas covering an uneven boxing ring.

This was now my home.

5

Rocky Marshmallow

I WAS IN the right place at the right time. Her name was Stella and when she walked through the doors of the gym in the Royal Orchid Hotel in Chiang Mai city centre, everybody stopped what they were doing. She looked out of place with her long, flowing, black hair, expensive clothes and Jackie Onassis sunglasses. She walked confidently around the gym; she was wearing dark blue denim jeans tucked into brown, knee-high boots, and spoke to all the non-Thais.

It turned out she was a casting agent looking for extras for a movie they were filming in Chiang Mai. Was I interested? Of course I was!

The film was the fourth in the Rambo series, to be called simply Rambo. The star, of course, was Sylvester Stallone, known to his friends as Sly. As I stood there in a pool of sweat, this woman stepped back and coolly appraised me. "Hey, honey, what's your name?" I was surprised, she had a strong American accent and carried herself with the sort of American confidence I wasn't used to seeing in a Thai woman.

"Billy, Billy Moore."

"OK, Billy, I need some details. How tall are you?"

"Five eight."

"And your weight?"

"94kg."

"Do you have a number I can contact you on?"

"Yes," I said and gave her my mobile number.

"OK, just one more thing and we're done. I need a picture. Can you stand over there and hold up this placard?" I felt like I was standing on an ID parade. One of the usual suspects again, I thought ruefully.

She promised to call me and then left. I dismissed the whole thing and almost forgot about it until I received a call two weeks later. I was to be at the front entrance of the Grand Hotel at 4.00am. My job was to play Stallone's stunt stand-in.

At the appointed time, Stella was there and showed me and a few others to waiting vans, which would take us to a secret jungle location close to the Burmese border.

MaMe was stunning; she looked like a superstar and, in fact – unknown to me – she really was a star here in Thailand. She had been in many films and was quite famous. I liked MaMe immediately, she was down-to-earth and didn't make you feel beneath her; to her everyone was equal. She was keen to improve her English, so I told her that I had a TEFL certificate. Maybe I should have kept quiet because from then on she treated me as her English teacher. It was fun and each time we travelled to our location we would sing songs. She especially liked a certain number by John Denver and sang "I'm leaving on a jet plane, don't know when I'll be back again," every day until I was fed up with hearing the tune and wanted to kill John Denver.

MaMe had the opportunity to play a part in Rambo but she wasn't interested. She had come along only to help out her friends Stella and Noi with casting.

Sly Stallone was huge. He looked like John Rambo and Rocky Balboa rolled into one. I was on unit one and worked close to Sly. Kevin King was his right-hand man and, as luck would have it, like me he was from Liverpool.

Kevin had seen a video clip of me boxing and wanted to show it to Sly. It was a classic clip of me winning by a second-round KO. I could see Sly nodding as he watched the clip on my digital camera.

"He's dead impressed with that, lad. He likes all that," said Kevin as he handed me back my camera. "Look, we need to crack on and get this movie rolling," he said and walked off into the jungle.

You wouldn't believe the parts of your body that mosquitoes can bite. By the end of a long day's filming in the hot, thick and humid jungle, I would find bites in the most unusual places – ears and toes, even my balls had been chewed on. The bottles of Deet mosquito spray the crew and I went through should have been enough to kill every mosquito in the whole country.

After work on the glamorous Hollywood film set, I left that fantasy world one day and returned for the evening to the hard, stark reality of the Muay Thai arena. I had to get ready to fight again.

This time, Papa wanted me to change my name. He said I should have a nickname for when I'm fighting.

"What like?" I asked him.

"Boom Boom," Papa immediately answered.

"Boom Boom?" I questioned.

"Yes, you boom boom lady too much, HIV no good," Papa spat.

What could I say? I was young, single, and horny and in a country where relationships could be instantaneous. "I love you, sexy man. What your name?" was the chat-up line used by every bar girl, many of them beautiful women. I am an addict in more ways than one. I had to have everything right now. I despised the slow courting process, the wining and dining, the spending of time and money, the effort it took. For what? A kiss on the cheek at the end of the night! I guess I was lacking something in the art of romance.

"Don't worry, Papa, I never leave home without them," I said, winking and waving a packet of Trojan condoms in the air, like it was the winning lottery ticket.

"Aye heeya!" (animal) he said, smiled and shook his head.

"You big movie star now, Locky. Many lady love you."

"Yeah, Rocky Marshmallow," I muttered to myself.

"OK, tonight you big fight, Boom Boom. You ready?"

This was going to be my toughest fight ever, against a hard-head named Eckachai Sommai. He was a champion, a real warrior with over 200 battles to his name. A few of the guys I worked with on the set came along to offer me their support.

The fight was a war that went the distance, with me winning on points. Papa wasn't happy and didn't want to pay me because he had expected me to win by a KO. He saw the look of disappointment on my face as I pointed out that I couldn't knock out everyone I fought, and anyway, Eckachai Sommai was one of my best opponents and he deserved the respect I had given him at the end of the contest.

"I pay you this one time. Next time you knock out," Papa begrudgingly conceded.

"What happened, lad? Your head looks like a box of oranges," Kevin King asked me the next day on set.

"Muay Thai. I had a fight last night."

"Did you win?"

"Yeah, just about, but the arsehole didn't want to pay me."

"What! Why's that then?"

"Because I didn't knock the guy out."

"Yeah well, he's right, you should have knocked him out," he said, laughing. "You've got some bruises there. Look at the state of your ears. Come over here. I want Sly to see this." We both walked over to Stallone, who was standing alone, chewing on an expensive cigar while admiring the jungle scenery.

"Sly, take a look at this," said Kevin, pointing at the multiple bruises around my face. "He boxed one of those Thais last night and beat him on his own turf."

Sly slowly looked me up and down. "Hey, man, that's great. You're a warrior," he complemented me.

"Sly, Billy's always been a great fan of yours. Any chance of him and you getting a few photos together?"

"Sure, man, why not?" agreed Sly.

"Ah, nice one, Kev," I beamed, not believing this was happening. I handed him my camera and posed with Sly.

Kevin took a lot of pictures but decided the light wasn't right. "Let's go to my dressing room, it ain't so good out here," Sly said. We took some good pictures. Sly held his guard up in the classic pugilistic pose and encouraged me to do the same. Kevin was flashing away like David Bailey. After we had finished, I left Sly's dressing room.

Outside, I bumped into Yannie who idolised Stallone and who had been trying to get a picture with him since day one. "Wow, man, you're so lucky. You think I could get a picture? Please, Billy, speak to your friend Kevin," begged Yannie.

"I don't know, mate. I had to get me head punched in for that picture," I said.

"Really? Wow, man, who do I get to punch my head in?" Yannie asked me. I could see he was serious. Yannie was obsessed with Stallone; he was from Australia and had travelled half-way round the world to be an extra in the movie. He was tall, dark and handsome with long, black curly hair. Rather than walk around like everyone else, he stalked Sly. He started wearing red bandanas and talking like his hero: "Yo, Paulie, tell Adrian she ain't so bad." To some, his bad impersonation of Rocky was funny, but most of us thought he was creepy. I guess that's why he didn't get much work on set. He didn't have many friends.

"Hey, Billy, can I come and join you down at the arena? Maybe I could get a fight with one those guys you train with?" Yannie asked me.

"Have you ever boxed before?"

"Well, I've done taekwondo back home and watched Enter the Dragon about a million times," he said, as he kicked and chopped violently at the air in an impression of Bruce Lee.

"OK, I'll meet you at the CEC arena at about 9.00pm."

"CEC?" he asked, obviously confused.

"Yeah, you can't miss it. It's next to the night bazaar."

"You mean where the girlie bars are?"

"That's the place. See you there at 9.00pm, OK?"

Yannie turned up with a small sports bag. He changed into boxing shorts and began stretching next to the ring. Papa and the others looked on in amusement. "Billy, he want fight, yes?" Papa asked, rubbing his hands together greedily. "He pay money me OK!"

"No, he'll fight for tips, same same me," I said.

Yannie was surrounded by about five of the young boxers who all seemed to want to be the one to fight him. Lae was about the same size and weight as Yannie and a perfect sparring partner for him. "Go easy on him, OK, Lae?"

"No problem, Mr Billy."

"OK, Yannie, you're up next. Just follow what Lae does and you'll be OK," I said.

"Hey, this is great. Do you think Stallone will be impressed?" he asked, looking like a big kid on Christmas Day.

"Yeah, maybe. Don't forget to keep your hands up when you're in there," I warned him.

The two fighters who were in the ring had just finished performing the ram muay (traditional Muay Thai dance). Yannie looked on, watching this ritual dance, concentration etched on his face.

"OK, mate, are you ready? Don't worry, I'll be in your corner," I said, handing him some water before his show bout. "Remember it's not for real; just a show," I reminded him.

Yannie held onto the top rope and jumped easily over into the ring. His opponent, Lae, was already waiting. The ritual hypnotic Thai music began. Lae swayed left and right gently, raising his legs in all four directions. Everybody watched, stunned as Yannie started to flap his arms about like a bird preparing for flight.

"Billy, what he do? Kon ba!" (he's crazy) said Papa. Yannie was now on one knee, punching the air slowly and gently bouncing his other leg up and down to the music's beat. He was trying to perform the ram muay but looked like he was swatting flies. Papa laughed out loud. "His name what?" he asked between sniggers.

"Yannie."

"Fanny?"

"No, never mind; call him Rambo, he'll like that."

"OK, lady and gentlemen, tonight we big fight. In red corner, champion boxer from Thailand, fight Rambo from…" Papa paused. "Where he from?"

"Australia."

"…Australia," he shouted loudly into the microphone.

Yannie performed terribly, and spent more time running away from Lae than actually fighting him. But he did help collect tips and as he was also short of money, I asked Papa to give him a share of what was collected.

I was amazed to note Sly's professionalism as he got in character for a scene. His chest was pumped out and his massive muscles rippled. He looked like he was on the warpath. "What's up with him, Kev? He doesn't look happy," I said.

"He's getting ready to kill someone in the next scene. He's going to rip his throat out," said Kevin, pointing at a guy dressed in Burmese military attire.

"Look, I'm not being funny, but is it actually possible to rip out a person's throat with your bare hands? I mean, no human being can do that, can they?"

"Rambo can!" Kevin said with conviction.

"Action!" Bill, the assistant director, shouted.

I watched as Sly took hold of the smaller guy's throat and squeezed, his face contorted in sheer hate for this little man. He pulled hard, tearing away a layer of latex skin, and making the fake blood pump out and pour down the soldier's uniform.

"Cut!" said Bill. Sly wasn't happy with the lights and wanted to go again.

"I need a volunteer. Who wants to get his throat ripped out?" Sly asked the small crowd, his eyes fixing on me.

"I don't mind," I volunteered, and moved myself into position in front of Sly.

I felt his huge hands grip me around my throat. He was so close, I could feel the breath from his nostrils on the back of my neck. Once the crew sorted out the lights and Sly was eventually happy, the scene was finished in one take. "Right," he said, "what's next?"

Over the next few months' filming I found myself teetering across dangerous waterfalls, wading knee-deep in muddy water, sitting in bamboo cages and being eaten alive by huge red ants.

The filming was coming to an end and people were leaving to go home. I said my goodbyes sadly to Kevin and a few of the others I had become close to. Yannie had his bags packed and was on the next flight to LA to be closer to his hero. "Yo, Yannie, you ain't so bad," I said, doing my best Rocky impersonation for him.

"You ain't so bad yourself," he said before leaving.

That was the last time I saw him. With everyone gone I felt lost. What do I do now? I had had structure in my life for the past seven months; it had given me a sense of belonging, of being needed. It was time I took control of my life and stayed on a positive path.

I found a job teaching English at a language centre on the outskirts of Chiang Mai. It was a pretty shabby outfit, run by a bunch of cowboys. They didn't even ask me if I had a criminal record. All they saw was the TEFL certificate, the smart pants, the red striped shirt and blue tie. The hours were long and the money wasn't much but it kept me busy and the language centre was close to where I lived.

I met a wonderful guy whilst working on the Rambo set. Matt Marsden was a tall, good-looking man who had worked on the long-running British TV soap Coronation Street for a year before breaking loose and heading for Los Angeles. There, his acting talent and Hollywood looks landed him a part in the movie Black Hawk Down.

From the success he achieved on that film, he attracted the interest of Hollywood moguls keen to employ such a talented young up-and-coming English actor. Matt had continued to move forward with his career and had earned a prominent role in Rambo.

Before Matt finished filming he came to the language centre where I was working and took time away from his busy schedule to chat to the young Thai students I taught. He talked about his acting career and answered questions from each of the young students. There was none of the Hollywood star about him; he was assured and unassuming and I was grateful for his support and interest.

My Thai students will never forget his visit that day, and will no doubt be telling their families for years to come of the day a young Hollywood star came to meet them in college and answer their questions. We became good friends and continue to remain in contact even today.

Boxing in the evenings kept me fit and helped me with the bills. Mama wanted to know when I was going to find a good woman and settle down. "You same butterfly," she said. "You fly here, you fly there, you no happy one place, na," she said, flapping her arms dramatically. "Pooying dee dee ha yack, chai mai?" (Is a good woman hard to find?)

I had by this time seen and experienced many beautiful women, but one in particular was the most beautiful I had ever seen. Her hair was the colour of honey, her dark brown eyes were like two huge lakes on a cool summer night and she smelled of freshly baked blackberry muffins on a cold winter morning.

I fell in love with her heart-shaped face and painted red lips. I was totally blown away, convinced I was in love or, at least, well on the way. When I plucked up the courage to ask her out I felt like a teenager taking his first love to the cinema.

Little did I know then what life had in store for me.

6

Relapse

IF YOUR NEXT-DOOR neighbour was a mass murderer you would want to know everything about him, correct? Where does he go? Who are his friends? What time does he sleep? Eat? Exercise? You would want to know absolutely everything, and would be constantly aware of his movements at all times because, maybe, if you dropped your guard, he would creep up behind you and split open your skull with an axe, killing you instantly.

Only my neighbour is not a crazy axe murderer and he's not out to destroy me. But I do live with a murderer and that murderer is inside me. He lives in my head and he wants to kill me the first chance he gets. He's waiting for me to drop my guard. He's always ready to pounce at the first sign of weakness. But he won't kill me with an axe or a gun – his weapon of choice is drugs.

He is a sadistic bastard and wants to kill me slowly, revelling in my misery, thriving on my feelings. He's cunning, powerful and baffling. He is the worst enemy I have ever encountered. Alone I am in bad company.

Rule number 1: Be vigilant! Don't forget what will happen to you if you let down your defences.

Rule number 2: Don't fall in love with a Thai woman. It's destined to fail, especially with the reputation such ladies have for breaking hearts as well as your bank balance.

I thought I could tame Goy. I say "tame" because to me Thai women were wild, beautiful creatures. But I told myself that she was different, that she was not some sleazy bar girl. Actually, Goy was educated, had been to university and had never even seen the inside of a bar. Her family was not poor and had a healthy rice crop from their farm in Phayao, just north of Chiang Mai.

She had to be the right woman this time, didn't she? Wrong! This sweet, innocent, soft-talking woman turned out to be a liar and a cheat. She had a Thai boyfriend tucked away in Bangkok. Goy and her like are unequalled, professional bullshitters, out to milk you dry. It's true; we foreigners are just walking dollar symbols to them.

"Billy, I love you same same him." LOVE! What did this woman know about love?

"How can you love two men?" I asked her, obviously upset.

I had to go to Burma to renew my visa, and she had to go to Bangkok to see her other boyfriend or geek (sex buddy).

"I go now, please no be angry," she said, tears brimming in her large, soft brown eyes.

Angry? I was pissed. Over the last few years, I had begun to discover that I had feelings which burnt deep inside me, and I was unable to express them for fear of showing weakness. I knew this was rejection, and for the first time I discovered that I really hated rejection. Leaving her crying and unable to say anything, I grabbed my keys, jumped on my sports bike, and drove at top speed to the Thai-Burmese border.

My sleek black sports bike, a Honda 150 CBR, was my prized possession. I bought it for 60,000 baht, brand new, using the money I had earned on Rambo.

I drove like crazy. I was clad from head to toe in black, which suited my mood, and the further I drove, the more the memory of Goy faded behind me. In reality, I knew I was running away once again, from my feelings and from my emotions. Also once again, I was alone.

I was still feeling pissed and sorry for myself as I crossed the bridge into Burma, followed by a pack of young Burmese glue sniffers, begging me for any spare change. I ignored them and made my way into the bustling marketplace where I was surrounded by traders selling everything from counterfeit CDs to Viagra and cheap cigarettes.

I walked around aimlessly, wondering what to do. I couldn't shake the feelings I had hanging over me, suffocating me. Every breath I took was like a knife ripping at my heart. I felt shabby, rejected like a cheap, used suit on the scrap heap.

A couple of young Burmese boys who were selling fake-brand cigarettes came towards me.

"You want cheap cigarette, mister?"

"I no smokey," I told them.

"You want lady?"

A woman was the last thing I wanted as I couldn't get Goy out of my head. She had betrayed me with her lies and now I felt stupid and foolish that I had believed her. How naive I was to allow myself to fall in love. I went through every emotion possible, from the initial shock to disbelief, denial and anger to self pity, back to anger then finally hatred.

"Hey, mister, we have sexy lady," said the boy, dragging me away from my thoughts. He pulled out an old tattered brochure and thrust it towards my face.

"No! No lady!" I looked him straight in the eyes and heard a disembodied voice speak.

"I want drugs!"

I recognised the voice. It was mine. The moment I had dreaded, the moment I had fought against for so long, had come back full circle to haunt me.

I had just pressed my self-destruct button.

The boy looked at me very confused, not understanding why I was acting this way.

"Heroin!" I said slowly.

"Heroin? Pong kao? Have. Follow me!" he said excitedly.

We walked out of the marketplace towards a motorcycle taxi rank next to a small building. The boy told me to follow him and we went up some stairs to a coffee shop where the smell of freshly cooked food filled the air. I sat down while the boy went to the corner of the darkened room to speak to a group of older men.

I was nervous. What was I doing here? I ordered a coffee; it was strong and sweet. The boy came back and showed me a bottle with an orange cap that he said contained five grams of pure, unadulterated China White.

"500 baht, mister."

This was crazy! It was madness! But that's where my head was. I'd crossed the line; there was no turning back now. I had taken a step back into the past, and my palms were sweaty with anxiety. I reached for the bottle and handed him the money. If I ever needed more stuff I could meet him under the bridge on the Thai side.

I made my way across the border into Thailand, fear sweating out of my pores every step of the way. I collected my visa, had it stamped for another month and jumped back on my bike.

I was in Chiang Mai within two hours and sitting at a bar with a double Jack Daniels. The heroin was still in my shorts, untouched. I had a battle going on inside me. I kept thinking, "FUCK IT, FUCK IT ALL!" What was the point anymore? Every fibre of my being screamed out: drink the FUCKIN' whiskey!

Relationships weren't my only problem. It was life on life's terms that was affecting me, not some break-up with a woman I hardly knew. Just being me was a problem, I couldn't blame Goy or anyone else for what I was about to do.

I lifted the whiskey to my lips. I just wanted the pain I was feeling to go away. I knew this wasn't the answer. "FUCK IT, MAN," I said aloud and took a huge swig. The back of my throat burned and an involuntary shiver ran down my spine.

I emptied the glass and ordered another. I pulled out my phone and called Marty, a British guy I knew. He answered on the fourth ring.

"Hello, mate, what's going on?" he asked.

I explained the situation I now found myself in. He told me to sit tight and that he would be with me in ten minutes.

Marty arrived when I was on my third Jack Daniels and feeling the effects; he joined me for a drink and listened to me moan and whinge about my problems. In my increasingly drunken state I wanted to burn Goy's mother's house down. I ranted that I wanted to hurt her like she had hurt me. Once the drink had hit my lips, my world speed-balled. I wanted to keep on drinking until I fell into a stupor just like all my obsessions.

My mood changed. I wanted to go clubbing and I wanted cocaine. Marty wasn't sure he could score but told me the ladyboys on Soi 2 of Loi Kroi might be able to help.

As we parked our bikes in Soi 2, a small ladyboy in red high heels approached us. He had long, straight, black hair and a pair of huge tits.

"Hello, sexy man. I May. You like me?" said the tranny.

Marty asked about buying cocaine.

"No have. You like ya ba, sexy man? I have."

Neither of us had heard of this drug. The ladyboy told us it was methamphetamine in tablet form and would cost us 250 baht a pill. Later on, we discovered the real price; the bastard had robbed us of 50 baht every time we bought from him, and with my obsessive intake he was making a Thai fortune.

"Make you many happy," May said as he jumped on the back of Marty's bike. I followed them to a run-down apartment block close to the main train station.

May showed us into a room on the second floor and introduced us to Nok, an attractive young woman in her mid-twenties. I counted five other men in the room, all Thais, seated on the floor playing cards. The room was small and thick with cigarette smoke.

"Sit down, please," said Nok, pointing to an old battered double bed in the corner of the room. May took our money and left. Nobody spoke. The Thais didn't even acknowledge our presence, they just played their card game, concentration etched on their hard young faces. May returned and handed me a couple of red pills with the letters WY inscribed on them.

"What are these? Ecstasy tablets?" I asked May.

"No same, this ya ba. Very good!"

I was an addict. I thought I had seen every drug available on the market, but obviously not. May produced a small piece of foil, quickly made a paper tube, placed the pill on the foil and gently waved a flame under it. I watched as the smoke began to rise.

May inhaled the smoke through the tube, held it in his lungs then exhaled.

"OK, now you," he said, handing me the foil. The red pill was now gone, and in its place was a blob of black oil similar to the beetle you would find when smoking heroin, except that this had little white crystals forming on top. May helped me by gliding the lighter under the foil; I could smell his cheap perfume as I inhaled the white smoke.

Once my lungs were full, I raised my hand to halt him. I held in the smoke for about twenty seconds before releasing it. My heart was suddenly pounding and I felt detached from my body; this was some kind of super speed with an intense rush. I craved more, and smoked another five of these small pills within the space of an hour.

Marty, who had shared his pills with Nok, was now sitting on the floor with the rest of the Thais, smoking and playing cards. He had the same intense expression on his face that the others had when I first came into the room. I was not interested in playing cards. I still had the heroin and money.

I paid for more pills, then left the room to embark on a journey that would take me to the very depths of HELL!

7

Ya Ba

YA BA! METHAMPHETAMINE, the crack cocaine of South East Asia. When translated, ya ba means crazy drug. It also has other names: WY, horse and tiger. It has a sweet smell not unlike perfume. It's cheap and easy to produce, but if you're caught supplying this drug, the maximum penalty in Thailand is death.

I quit my job teaching at the language centre as my mind was preoccupied and I was incapable of offering a proper education to Thai teenage students. I was back in the grip of addiction; almost all of my savings were spent on buying ya ba. I was hooked after that first hit with May, and couldn't get enough. My body screamed for more. My life turned upside down and was now in total chaos.

Most days I would hang about the gym with some of the other Thai boxers and drink the same cheap whiskey. Some smoked ya ba and I would join them to get high before show fights. Mama would look at me sadly while shaking her head. "Billy, ya ba no good!" I would look away, avoiding eye contact as I felt ashamed, but I also laughed and told her not to worry, because I could handle it.

I would continue to box in the evenings and entertain the visiting tourists; they saw me as a novelty, something new to watch. They loved to see a fight between a foreigner and a Thai. I would guarantee the expectant crowd a real show. In this self-destructive mood I just wanted to inflict pain on my opponent and the world. The crowds wanted blood and bruises; that's what they came to see. This is also what paid my bills.

So, as long as the punters didn't feel cheated, the tips were good. Unfortunately, some evenings were bad and we wouldn't even make enough money for a bowl of noodles. Papa would get me a big fight once a week and this would be enough to cover my monthly rent and other living expenses, but it was still not enough for my growing ya ba habit.

Pi Nong, an ex-Thai Police officer and boxer, fought for the club inside the Bar Beer Centre, opposite Thapae Gate, Chiang Mai. He was a big, stocky fellow with a huge neck, strong legs and the battered face of a fighter. He looked very intimidating, and had a swagger on him like he owned the world. He had heard from Nimdam that I was looking to score ya ba, and wanted to get in on some of the action. Nimdam told me he was cool, but I was suspicious. After all, this arsehole was police, or at least he used to be.

Pi Nong invited me to his brother's room at the back of the Bar Beer Gym. The brother, Tong, produced a small bag of pills.

"Relax," he said, smiling and showing me a mouth full of black, rotted teeth. He handed me one of the pills to test, and they were good.

I had a bit of back-up money tucked away for a rainy day. He told me he could get me ya ba cheaply if I bought it in bulk.

"You can make good money; you sell to farang no problem, up to you."

I didn't want to sell drugs, just use them.

I took his number and said I'd let him know.

Spicy, a popular night club in Chiang Mai, was a dumping ground for bar girls and lonely foreigners, and this is where I met Scott. Scott was a thirty-something from London who had lived in Chiang Mai for the past three years. He had been down on his luck since he lost his bar in Phrae, about 150km from the city. He had a heroin habit as well as a ya ba problem. He told me that he and his girlfriend would sell the pills if I could get them. So I gave Pi Nong a call to meet up, and told Scott I would be back in half an hour. I then made my way over to the Bar Beer Centre and paid Pi Nong 40,000 baht for 500 ya ba pills.

This was it. Every baht I possessed was gone. There was now no going back.

I waited as Pi Nong greedily counted my money and then headed back to Spicy and Scott, riding my bike carefully to avoid any suspicion from the police.

Scott was waiting for me in the toilets at the back of Spicy, and I handed him 100 pills.

"These are for now; 200 baht each, OK?" I was making 120 baht on every tablet I sold Scott which

I am sure would make him his profit. I also gave him about one gram of heroin that was left from my previous trip to Burma.

"You can have this too, OK, mate?"

"What is it?"

"I think it's China White."

"Yeah, where did you get it?"

"In Burma."

"Burma? So why the hell is it called China White, then?"

"I don't know. What's with all the questions? Just smoke it."

"Nice one, Bill," he said, shaking my hand and promising to call me once the ya ba was sold.

The music system inside Spicy was pumping out loud hip hop. The dance floor was heaving with young Thai bar girls who were clinging onto farangs or cheap bottles of beer. I left the club alone and headed home.

I got a call from Scott the next day with good news. He had sold all of the pills and wanted more. This pleased me; it looked as if I was going to make a tidy profit. He wanted to know if I could get him more heroin.

"That was dynamite, Bill, it was the bollocks." It was the best shit he had ever had.

He could get me 3,000 baht a gram. That was good money, and all I had to do was contact my Thai connections on the Muay Thai scene, pay for the ya ba and pass it on to Scott. The heroin I would score myself from Bo, in Burma, every couple of weeks.

Pi Nong was a bully and was feared by most of the boxers in and around the city. He spent all of his money on cigarettes and whiskey, so he constantly pestered me for cash and for some of the pills that I was getting from his brother, Tong.

I felt obliged to help him since, of course, it was he who'd put me in contact with Tong in the first place.

Pi Nong would call my phone or turn up uninvited at my apartment door at all hours. He would demand, beg and plead that I help him. He was becoming trouble. I gave him money and pills, hoping it would keep the peace and he would leave me alone. He reminded me of a stray dog. I had to be careful – if I kept feeding him, he would keep coming back.

The more ya ba I smoked the more paranoid I became. I didn't feel safe, so I asked Pi Nong if he could get me a gun. Every man and his dog carried a gun in Thailand. He got me a brand new Colt 45; it was cheap at 10,000 baht.

As my drug-fuelled paranoia increased, my room became full of weapons. I had a samurai sword, a machete and even a knuckle-duster. Now I had a Colt 45 pistol to add to my collection.

I often locked myself in my room with a couple of bar girls and smoked ya ba endlessly. Scott would call round to drop off money and pick up more pills. I would only venture out of my apartment during the early hours of the morning, with Pi Nong close by, following behind like a lap dog.

I knew that being involved in drugs was a dangerous game. I was deeply addicted and found it impossible to stop. I was so close to Tong, the main dealer, that I was making good profits. I saw myself as a middleman and didn't want to get my hands dirty. I was careful and changed my phone and sim card once a week. As my paranoia increased, I had strong feelings of being watched, or followed. Fortunately I was able to shake these feelings off, and I convinced myself that it had to be the ya ba.

I hid huge amounts of drugs in the alley behind my apartment block. I couldn't sleep, my weight dropped rapidly and dark rings appeared around my eyes. I looked like an anorexic panda and lived the life of a vampire. All the money, women, and fancy clothes I had meant nothing.

I began to believe I was bullet-proof, one of the untouchables. I thought I was too clever for the police. I never carried drugs on my person, was never involved in selling them to the public and kept a low profile. Not many people were aware of my lifestyle. The few who were were Pi Nong, Scott and Scott's girlfriend. Even though they needed me, I still didn't trust them, especially Pi Nong. He was greedy and jealous of Scott. I started to ignore Pi Nong's calls and stopped answering the door when he knocked. I would park my sports bike a couple of streets away from my apartment. But still he would knock, shouting, "Billy! Billy! I want WY. I pay OK."

This was all bullshit, a ploy to get me to answer the door. I needed a break from it all and had a visa run coming up: I had to leave Thailand and come back in to renew my visa. So I decided to take a trip to Laos and spend a couple of days away from the paranoia, somewhere I was unknown and could be anonymous.

8

Laos

LAOS, PART OF which is included in the notorious Golden Triangle, is a landlocked country bordered by China, Vietnam, Thailand, Burma and Cambodia. I had scored! The ya ba was cheap here in Laos, much cheaper than in Thailand, and of better quality, too. I had bought about one thousand pills and a small amount of opium, enough to get the death sentence or at least life in prison, but I was past caring. I wasn't the Billy who had turned his life around and had achieved goals and dreams beyond his wildest imagination. That person was now gone. In his place lurked someone evil, dark and frightening. The only person I ever feared was myself. I knew the destruction I was capable of creating while under the influence of drugs.

I decided to go clubbing. I was here for the weekend and didn't have to be at the Thai embassy until noon on Monday to pick up my visa. I rented a Honda Wave 100cc motorbike and headed to Don Jan Palace, a roof-top night club close to the Mekong, the huge river that separates Thailand from Laos. People say that Laos resembles Thailand twenty years ago. The whole country seemed to switch off and sleep at 11pm. Don Jan's was the only place that stayed awake.

The only problem was that I was also half-asleep, stoned on the local weed and spaced out on ya ba. I didn't make it to the night club. A chorus of "hello, sexy man" from a couple of ladyboys by the roadside made me lose concentration for a second or two and I smashed my scooter straight into two on-coming bikes.

I bounced along the road like a rag doll, simply thrown everywhere, my back scraping along the gritty road. I was lucky my head didn't come into contact with any of the on-coming traffic that swerved to avoid smashing up more of my battered body. Suddenly I came to a halt; I was flat on my back and staring up into the cool night sky. Nothing seemed to be working, my breathing was all wrong, in fact it was like I had forgotten how to inhale and exhale. I looked around and could see people milling about. Torch lights were shining into my face, cars and bikes stopped close by and came to a halt all around me, but all I could remember was the cold silence. I could see lips moving but I heard nothing. There was movement all around me, yet all that remained was the silence.

I was badly smashed up. So bad, in fact, that I thought I was going to die. I looked up and saw a small crowd looking down at me. I wanted to scream "please help me!" but I couldn't form the words. Why weren't these people helping me?

The next thing I can recall was the stink of cheap Mekong whiskey in my face and an English-speaking voice saying, "Jesus, are you OK, mate? Hang in there; I'm going to get you help."

I felt arms grip me, lifting me up; the pain in my chest was immense. Asian faces were all around me. Someone poured salt water down my throat, which caused me to gag and scream out in pain. Why they did this, I had no idea.

"Get away! Leave me alone!"

They were shouting in a language I couldn't understand; it was nothing more than babble. I just wanted to get away as their help was killing me.

I heard shouts in a language I understood. "Get off him; you're going to kill him, you eejits." It was a Westerner. I recognised his accent as southern Irish, probably Dublin.

"Don't worry, mate, I'm Paddy. We'll get you to hospital."

I was on my way to Moho Sut Hospital on the floor of a tuk tuk. I was losing blood fast and finding it difficult to breathe. It was a bumpy journey in the back of that tuk tuk. We finally arrived at the hospital where I was lumbered into a wheelbarrow and rushed into the Emergency Room. I was helped onto a bed, each movement causing a huge pain to rush through my chest. All I could do was grit my teeth and hold on.

Laos is an extremely poor, third-world country. I looked around the hospital room. It had dirty whitewashed walls and absolutely no modern technology. It was pretty basic. Paddy was speaking to me when two soldiers entered, carrying sub-machine guns, scary looking weapons with banana clips.

My first thought was "SHIT!" I suddenly remembered I still had the ya ba pills in my pocket. A thousand questions ran through my mind. Did they know? Had the taxi driver, who supplied me with the drugs, informed on me? I was afraid. They said nothing, they just stared at me until they produced a camera and took a photo of me, and then left. Relief swept over me.

By this time my breathing was becoming easier. I heard Paddy speaking to a doctor who was wearing a dirty, blood-stained jacket and carried a bottle of beer with him. Paddy was telling the doctor to remove something from my left side. It turned out to be a brake lever which had imbedded itself in my body, puncturing my stomach wall.

Paddy kept talking to me. "How are you, mate? Do you speak English?"

I managed to croak in reply: "I'm OK! Please just get me out of here,"

"Are you sure?" he enquired.

I wasn't, but feared the soldiers would come back again. The doctor took my money, pumped me full of morphine, patched me up, and helped me to a waiting taxi.

Paddy took me to his home, a small apartment in the city. It would be another two days before I would be able to collect my visa, leave the country, and seek better medical care.

When I returned to Thailand I found out how serious my injuries were. I had two broken ribs, a punctured left lung, internal bleeding and major abdominal injuries.

I used more and more ya ba to ease the pain. This was insanity, total insanity! My mind and thinking were centred around using drugs to release me from both the internal and external pain I was feeling. I could have died that night, and wouldn't have cared as long as I'd had one last hit before the big sleep.

What kept me going were the drugs. I was pumped up on ya ba and huge amounts of morphine. I sold more drugs to help pay my ever-increasing medical bills. I didn't feel the pain. I had buried them deep, both physically and mentally.

Scott continued to get rid of the drugs but he began taking the piss. He would switch his phone off when I needed my money and when I did see him he would turn up short; I had to suffer his bollix just to get paid. He was smashing the heroin big time, and doing methadone as well as the ya ba. He and his junkie girlfriend were a problem to work with, but I had no choice.

Pi Nong didn't give a shit about anyone but himself. Even his wife and kids hated him. I had moved apartments three times, but this good-for-nothing bum must have had a built-in GPS – no matter where I moved, he would find me. I suspected Scott's girlfriend was feeding him information. Pi Nong was a proper ponce, in fact if there was a poll he would be voted King of the Ponces.

I liked him and hated him at the same time, maybe because I could see myself in him. He would be in my corner as long as the money and pills were available. I wasn't scared of him, but he had this aura surrounding him that was more of an attraction than fear. He was never violent, but totally the opposite, a real quiet guy, someone who would just sit there and observe everything around him.

"Who told you I lived here?" I was angry that he had found me yet again. "Was it that slag, Joy?" I said, not expecting him to tell me the truth. I would have to speak to Scott about her.

"Billy, you no like I, na," he said with a puppy-dog look. "Me help you, me friend you," he said in an audible whisper. I was just a walking pound note to the likes of him.

"You only come here to bum pills and money off me," I said bitterly. "You never once asked me how I was when I came back from Laos." I was pissed off with everyone. Nobody was for real in Thailand; friendships were fictitious. The real Thailand, the one that didn't smile, was a dangerous place to be. That's why I stayed – for the thrill and the excitement. The fantasy I could build here was of my own making.

I begrudgingly gave Pi Nong money and pills and told him not to come around again. He promised to stay away and only come if I needed him. That was difficult to believe and I knew that like a bad penny he would keep turning up.

Where the hell was Scott? He and his silly Thai chick were doing my head in. I phoned him hoping he would answer for once, but he didn't pick up. All I got was his voice mail.

I looked for Scott everywhere. He wasn't in his usual haunts, and I needed the money he owed me for more stock. I was outside his guest house at the ungodly hour of 3:00am. I was sure I would catch him either coming back home with Joy or hiding in his room.

His flat was on the third floor, room 301. The door to the main entrance was locked. I circled the building and found a drain pipe; if I climbed it I could swing over to the first floor balcony and quietly enter one of the rooms. I could then gain access into the corridor.

It was a simple plan and I executed it well. Within only a few minutes I was quietly heading towards the stairway so I could get to the third floor and to Scott's room. On the stairwell I heard movement; I froze and listened but heard nothing except my own breathing.

He pounced on me from behind the second floor exit door, screaming out in Thai. In his hand he had what appeared to be a gun. I immediately grabbed at both of his wrists and forced his arms above his head. I had no idea who he was but suspected he was either one of those rent-a-cops or building security.

This was all too much. I only wanted my money from Scott, not this, not wrestling with a Thai security guard wielding a handgun. I held the struggling man's arms above his head; I just wanted to get away so I lunged forward, raising my knee into his solar plexus and knocking the wind out of him. He dropped to the floor, but still he held onto his gun.

I was running down the stairs two at a time and could hear the security guard grunting and heaving a few flights above me; he wasn't fast enough. I was already at the door to the main entrance, but as I took hold of the handle and tugged on it, the door remained shut. It was a magnetic lock and would require a key fob to open it. In a mad panic, I looked around for another exit, but there was no time. The guard had fully recovered and was close behind me.

There was only one thing left for me to do; I would have to kick the glass door in, which made one hell of a noise as it shattered into a million pieces. I didn't care, I needed to get away, and just as I made it through the shattered glass door, the guard made a grab for me, but too late as I was now outside and running. Suddenly, I heard the loud crack of gun fire and felt bullets whizzing past my head.

I ran and ran until I could run no more, cursing Scott and his girlfriend all the way. Drugs, guns, hospitals and violence, this was just another day in paradise. I reached my apartment and tried Scott's phone one last time.

"Hellooo, who calling?" It was Scott's girlfriend; her whiny voice rattled my brain.

"It's Billy. Where the fuck's Scott?" I demanded, trying to control the rage I felt for this woman. She was trouble, it was written all over her.

"Billy, he sick, pong kao mai mee, na ka," she moaned about him not having any heroin.

"Look, tell him to come and see me. I'll make sure he's sorted."

She thanked me and waffled on about a load of shit. Buffalos and sick mothers were mentioned, the usual bullshit sob stories you hear every day in Thailand.

9

The Arrest

SCOTT WAS USING a lot of heroin, too much really. His girlfriend, Joy, a bar girl, was a known police informer and rumoured to have HIV. "I don't want you bringing your girlfriend round here, Scott. I don't trust her, understand?" I snarled, my face contorted to warn him of the consequences.

I needed him to move the pills. Scott had a lot of acquaintances, both foreign and Thai, so was in a position to move my stock of ya ba pills quickly.

"I need a line," he said desperately. Scott's hands were shaking. "I feel like shit." I handed him a bag of China White, the Devil's dust. Scott grabbed the bag and, with shaking hands, proceeded to set up a huge white line on my glass coffee table and snort the line greedily in one go.

"OK, mate, go easy. That stuff's rocket fuel," I told him. He looked up at me and beamed; his hands no longer shook, and his eyes had a dreamy faraway look. "Take the pills, and give me a call when you need more, and see what you can do with that gear." I threw him some of the heroin I had in my store cupboard and watched as he headed towards the door to leave.

"One more thing," I said. "Do yourself a favour and drop Joy. She's bad news, mate, everybody's talking about her."

He stopped, his hand on the door handle. Without looking back, he replied, "She's all I've got, Bill."

I couldn't believe he'd fallen in love with a Thai bar girl. He sounded lost, and the voice of a rejected soul screamed back at me, "I need her, Bill. I need someone."

His shoulders were hunched, his head leaning on the door. He was sobbing silently. I felt sorry for him. I knew how he felt. I was a regular visitor to those dark empty places. "Scott, slow down on the smack," I said, the pot calling the kettle black. He didn't answer, just walked out the door and closed it behind him. I liked Scott, but I wanted him to be careful.

I was alone in my room with nothing but my thoughts for company. I smoked some more ya ba. I hated thinking, I hated what I was, what I had become. The drugs wouldn't allow me to escape anymore.

The phone rang. It was Pi Nong. His name came up on my caller ID as "headache". I didn't want to answer the phone. This fat leech was trouble and I truly wished I had never met him.

I picked up the phone. "What is it?" I asked.

"My friend want WY. I come round in five minutes." He put the phone down before I could answer. What friend? This guy had no friends, the phone call from Pi

Nong made me feel uneasy. Maybe it was just the ya ba I had smoked; however, the feeling didn't go away.

I lived at a clean and respectable guesthouse off the beaten path about a mile outside the centre of Chiang Mai, facing the British Consulate. My room was on the top floor. You had to climb five sets of stairs before you reached my apartment. I opened my door and peered out to see if Pi Nong was on his way, only to be greeted by the sight of four armed men sprinting up the stairs.

"Shit." It was the police and they were already on the second floor. I quickly closed my door. There was no escape. I had to hide the pills and get rid of the cannabis that I had on the bedside cabinet. I grabbed the pills and forced them up my arse – over three hundred of them. I was glad they were wrapped in clingfilm.

I had the Thai stick weed in my hand. Somebody kicked the door. It held; the slide lock kept it secure, but I didn't know how long for. The weed was too big; like a tennis ball. I had no time to shove it up my arse. I had no choice but to hide it in my underwear.

"Police! Open the door!" Someone shouted. I instinctively sat with my back to the door in a forlorn attempt to prevent it from opening. Quickly, I scanned the room for anything I may have forgotten. It was then that I saw the gun. The Colt 45 was still on my bed and fully loaded. "Shit!" I had to think fast. I didn't want to die in a shootout. This wasn't the OK Corral and I definitely wasn't Clint Eastwood.

"OK, OK," I shouted.

"Open the door!" they ordered

"OK, but first show me some ID," I replied.

A card slid under my door. I picked it up. They were police. I opened the door and was pushed to the ground; guns were pointed at my head. I felt a foot on my neck.

"Hello, Rambo," I heard someone say. "You speak Thai?"

I did, but only a little, not enough to communicate under these circumstances, so I said, "No."

They handcuffed me and then searched the room. Somchai came towards me; I could see he had my gun in his hand. He leant down to where I was, lying face down on the floor and whacked me over the head with my own gun. So this was pistol whipping, I thought as a bright white light flashed across my eyes.

"Stop! Stop!" I pleaded as he continued to hit me about my head and body. The police were systematically going through my room and its contents, talking to each other and laughing at me. Suddenly they grabbed at my arms and body and heaved me to my feet saying nothing; they covered the handcuffs with a tee-shirt then dragged me out of my room and down the five flights of stairs to a waiting police car.

As I was pulled past the guesthouse reception desk, the manager looked in horror at the sight of one of his residents being escorted out of his premises in handcuffs. I looked away from his gaze, his face registering both shock and disbelief. Avoiding any form of eye contact with him, I faced the floor overwhelmed by shame.

The officers forced me into the back of the waiting police car. Two officers jumped in either side of me and with that I was taken on a short journey to the Ratchadamnoen Road police station.

My interrogation was underway.

They screamed at me in Thai as I sat in a chair, my cuffed hands behind my back. The room in the police station was small; a dim light hung by a chain from the ceiling and across the wall were cast tall shadows of the two officers staring at me. One I recognised from my arrest. He waved a thin piece of paper and shouted something. His partner unlocked my cuffs, then he handed me a pen and slammed the document down hard on the wooden table.

"You sign, na," he said quietly and smiled in a forlorn attempt to convince me he could be trusted. However, I had learnt what lay behind a Thai smile.

I looked at the document. It was written in Thai and I had no idea what it said.

"Mai kao jai," (I don't understand) I said, using one of the few words I knew in Thai, guessing the paper was a pre-written confession of my obvious guilt. He pointed to the array of weapons he had confiscated during the search of my room. On a small desk lay the Colt 45, the samurai sword, machete, a stun gun, my knuckle duster, a dozen or so cell phones and over 50 sim cards.

"You steal, na," he said, picking up one of the brand new Nokia phones.

"No!" I said, telling him the truth. I had bought them from a couple of Burmese junkies. Whether they had stolen them or not I didn't know. I wasn't going to be signing any piece of paper, that was for sure.

OK, the weapons and stolen phones were a problem. The ya ba was tucked away safe but the ganja was still in my underwear. I prayed to everyone – God, Allah, Buddha, the moon and stars – that the drugs wouldn't be compromised.

The officers seemed so pleased when they found the phones, I began to realise that this arrest wasn't about drugs. I am no Sherlock Holmes but I had worked that much out.

"You sign!" he demanded, pointing at the paper.

"Sign what? I've told you I don't understand."

"No problem, just your property," he said quietly.

Were they going to invent further charges? Send me to prison forever? The paper could have said anything.

"You steal black Honda motorbike?" he said, holding up my keys and waiving them in my face.

"No! It belongs to me, paid for with cash," I told him, which was true.

"You lie, William, sign here or you big trouble, na," he said, thrusting his pen towards me. I just remained silent. What was the point? They only believed what they wanted to believe.

There was a loud knock on the door. One of the police officers answered it, looked back at me and nodded to whoever was standing on the other side.

A small, balding man and a woman entered the room, he with a video camera set firmly on his shoulders and she with a clip board. She looked to be in her late twenties and had a very businesslike manner. Another guy with a camera came through the door and into the small room. It was becoming crowded.

"What's going on?" I was confused; a bright light from the video camera was shone into my eyes

"Smile, William, you on TV," laughed the cop who had been questioning me moments before. The TV crew asked me no questions and were gone in minutes. Later I found out that I had been paraded on national television and degraded in newspapers. Most of it was lies.

Once the door was closed, my hands were tightly cuffed behind my back again, cutting off the circulation and making them numb.

The two police officers continued to bombard me with questions. I could understand little of what they said. I heard them say Pi Nong's name but I remained quiet. They wanted to know where I had bought the phones; they mentioned the school I had worked for the year before. They knew a lot about me. I answered none of their questions nor signed their document.

Their anger and frustration grew. One of them picked up the machete and held it out towards me, shouting: "You answer, farang!" He then made a cutting motion across his throat and said, "Or you die."

I said nothing; I wasn't easily frightened and I had been in situations similar to this one before, only then it was in England – Liverpool in fact. I was young, probably about seventeen years old, and the local police (called the CID or also known as "Odds and Sods") grabbed me off the street. I prefer the word "kidnapped" because that's what they did. They kidnapped people. I was thrown in the back of an old Ford Sierra. They said they only wanted a chat, to gather information, but really they wanted to torture me. Who's selling drugs? Who's committing robberies? I didn't tell them anything, I was always proud of that fact; I wasn't a grass (a vital asset when living on the mean streets of Liverpool). They would have to use extreme force and they did. They twisted both of my wrists up behind me which caused excruciating pain. I screamed out loud. I spewed oaths and threats. I promised to kill their families and dogs and then begged them to stop. Tears streamed down my face.

"I don't know nothing," I told them. They knew I was lying and took me to a secluded spot in the south of Liverpool, a park, where they tried new tactics. The front passenger got out, opened the boot then returned carrying a dirty towel. Inside was a gun.

Now I didn't know much about guns then, but it was big, the kind Clint Eastwood used in the movie Dirty Harry. "Open your mouth, you little prick!" shouted the man with the gun. I kept it firmly closed. "Open your mouth, dickhead!" he roared. The big lump sitting next to me gave my wrist the good news, while the passenger grabbed my chin. I felt the barrel of the gun being forced past my lips, the cold steel entered my mouth, and I gagged violently. "We can kill you now and no one will know or even care."

I wasn't afraid; I knew I wasn't worth killing and if I died, so what! "Bang, bang you're dead."

They all broke into fits of laughter. "What we could do is let Mick here shag your arse," said the passenger pointing to the big lump sitting next to me. "Mick's gay and has Aids. Ain't that right, Mick?"

I didn't get raped, just kicked out of the car in the middle of nowhere. I just watched with bitter resentment as they drove away.

These earlier experiences of life in Liverpool had taught me that police were the same all over the world. They were just bullies, or a huge majority were. So I wasn't going to allow some jumped-up, under-paid, corrupt Thai police officer intimidate me.

"Fuck off!" I shouted. He grabbed me around the throat and throttled me. I couldn't breathe, my eyes felt like they were popping out my head. He screamed at me in Thai, then let go and stormed out of the room.

I lost track of the time. I didn't even know what day it was. Sometime later I was dragged out of the room and up some steps. I was shown a dark cell then shoved inside.

The heat was unbearable and the mass of stinking sweaty bodies invited a swarm of mosquitoes that mercilessly sucked and feasted on a buffet of blood. My sleeping space was on the floor next to the toilet which was raised off the floor so that the smell of piss and discarded food was above my head. It was filthy. Even the sewer rats that roamed the city would have been embarrassed to live in a place like this.

I had managed to conceal the ganja up my back passage, and boy did it hurt going up. I hadn't washed for days and my body was covered in angry red bites. I was hungry but couldn't eat. The food was rotten and there were bugs crawling all over the rice.

One of the Thai prisoners quietly tip-toed over to me and held out his hand, showing me a ball of sticky rice. "Eat, my friend, you no eat you sick." He was smiling and I could see genuine compassion in his eyes. I knew I had to eat.

10

The Lion's Den

THE POLICE TOOK me to the courthouse where I was remanded for twelve days into prison custody; there was no lawyer or any legal representation present at my hearing. The British Embassy had done nothing; they must have seen the TV coverage and read the papers, yet they made no attempt to see that I got a fair trial or the proper legal representation that I thought any British citizen was entitled to when abroad.

The holding cell I was placed in was brightly lit and had what looked to be about sixty other people inside. I could see that most of them were wearing a brown uniform of shorts and T-shirts and had fearsome looking chains around their ankles. I moved to a corner of the cell wanting to be alone. None of my family or friends knew where I was. Nobody was aware of my arrest. Feelings of despair crept over me; I was alone once again, with no hope of contacting anyone.

I lay back on the hard concrete floor and stared up at the flaky ceiling, thinking of the bad decisions I had made. "What if I had done this? Or what if I had done that?"

Then maybe I wouldn't have found myself in this horrible situation.

But it was too late now for the "what ifs and maybes." I was lost in my own thoughts for what seemed like hours. Then I heard shouts and sensed movement. The bus was here to take us to the prison. As I got to my feet, fear gripped me. What was I to expect? Would I be OK? The shouts got louder. I followed everyone else towards a gate, and handcuffs were placed on my wrists before I left the court to get on the bus.

The journey to the prison was short, no more than fifteen minutes. As we pulled up outside the massive gates of Chiang Mai prison I could see two huge stone lions, one each on either side of the main entrance, with bright red eyes, as if guarding what was beyond them. They looked terrifying. This was it! We were heading into the lion's den.

Once through the main entrance, we were hustled towards another gate leading into a compound. It was now dark and the compound was dimly lit, giving the prison an eerie feeling. We were all told to strip naked, and perform ten squats, holding our hands behind our ears in front of a guard. My arsehole was flapping like a busted fan belt, and my heart was banging against the walls of my chest. Although I was pretty sure the drugs would not be making an early appearance, still the fear remained.

My clothes were searched. I heard somebody speak in English. He was talking to me; he was smartly dressed, in blue shorts and a white T-shirt and wore an ID card around his neck attached to a silver chain. I assumed he was a guard or something, as he carried a baton and seemed to be ordering the prisoners about. He had hold of my jogging bottoms; he pulled out a sharp blade from the back of his shorts and cut off the legs. "Not allowed, shorts only," he told me.

We were all then marched to another area of the prison where we were told to bathe. The water was filthy and there was a thick film of dirt and scum on the surface. There was a bowl and, still naked, I scooped some of the disgusting water from the trough and poured it over my body. It had been days since I had washed so I made the most of it.

Once finished I put my dirty clothes back on, and followed the rest of the new prisoners a few yards to where metal plates and bowls were placed on the floor, with rice and a transparent-looking soup. Flies hovered above the dish. A scene from the movie Rambo First Blood flashed through my mind. It was the part where Colonel Trautman tells the local police that Rambo could survive anywhere, and could eat food that would make a belly pig puke. I doubted that even he would eat this swill. I was hungry so all I could do was grab a ball of sticky rice and stuff it into my mouth. The soup I couldn't touch.

We all then marched to the cell block and were shoved inside a cage. The room was big but not big enough for the seventy Thai prisoners it was holding.

As I walked in, I noticed the room had suddenly gone quiet as heads turned my way to look at the farang. I was nervous and scared at the same time but acted brave. The smell of human faeces was so strong I wanted to vomit.

Some of the inmates were squatting around bowls of sticky rice and a horrible brown soup. They were using their fingers to eat the food. These people were not clean, their clothes were torn and dirty. Some had filthy-looking blood-stained bandages covering their lower limbs. Wild thoughts flashed through my mind. I was horrified at what I was seeing.

"Oh shit," I cried out. HIV, and all the other horror stories you hear about in Thai prisons were running through my mind. The cell resembled a mass grave with arms and legs all over each other. I saw a motionless body on a damp, stained mattress, insects hovering over him. "My God," I thought, not believing what my eyes were seeing, "this cannot be happening. This isn't real. I must be hallucinating. Was he dead?" I asked myself. When I dared to look again, my worst thoughts were confirmed. Shit, he really was, the guy was dead.

"You sleep here, he no bite," said a ladyboy, patting the only available space in the cell. The guy who brought us to the room smiled and nodded in agreement. He pointed towards the dead body and said, "No problem. Tomorrow he go, many, many happy."

I was to sleep between a corpse and a ladyboy with big hands, big feet and a huge Adam's apple. This had to be the most putrid spot in the whole Thai kingdom.

"Sit! Sit, no be afraid, he die maybe two hour ago," said the tranny, painting his toenails as if this was an everyday occurrence. I looked over at the dead body. He had a scruffy old grey blanket covering his face. I looked around the room in disbelief. Everybody else was either deep in conversation or curled up sleeping. Nobody seemed concerned that we had a dead body locked in here with us.

I sat down with my knees pulled up to my chest.

"Hi, my name Tiffany. Your name is?" said the rough looking ladyboy. He had his long black hair tied back in a pony tail, full lips, a flat nose and a pock-marked face. He was young, probably mid-twenties. He was wearing pink shorts. His T-shirt was red and said in big, bold, black letters: "NO MONEY NO HONEY". I had no money so I guessed I wouldn't be getting any honey. "My name's Billy. You speak good English." I wasn't really surprised, as most of the ladyboys I had came across spoke English.

"I speak nit noy, only a little. You speak Thai, Billy?"

I could see he had no tits and probably had a ya ba habit. He was gaunt, and had scabs around his mouth.

"No."

Tiffany just smiled and pulled out a packet of cigarettes.

"You smoke?"

I was about to say no, but decided it wasn't a bad time to start again.

"What happened to him?" I said, pointing at the dead body.

"He heart no good. Old man smoke too much," said Tiffany, puffing away on his cigarette.

"I like your beautiful blue eye. You like sleep?"

I shook my head. I was exhausted but couldn't sleep.

"No worry, I no like farang, cock too big."

I laughed for the first time since I had been arrested and brought to this dreadful place. Tiffany told me what to expect whilst in prison, how during the day we would spend our time out in the exercise yard, in the scorching heat.

"What about a bed? What about food?" I asked, wondering why we were sleeping on the floor.

He said I would have to pay one of the other ladyboys the sum of 500 baht. They then would make a bed out of old blankets sewn together. And the prison shop sold food, if you had money.

"If no have no money, you eat food no good," said Tiffany.

I had no money. The police had taken my credit cards and, not surprisingly, even the money I had on me when I was arrested, had vanished.

The sound of a whistle silenced everyone and then the entire room stood. Tiffany grabbed my arm and pulled me up.

"National anthem! You have to stand," he whispered.

Everybody stood to attention, arms by their sides, and sang the Thai national anthem. It was over in minutes. Tiffany said this happened twice a day, at 8.00am and 6.00pm and was compulsory.

It was difficult to get comfortable; another whistle blew, this time it came from another cell.

"OK, 9.00pm. Everybody quiet, no talk, sleep OK!" said Tiffany, raising a finger to his lips.

"What about the lights?" I asked.

"Shush, they no go off, now sleep."

The fluorescents were powerful, bright, and the light hurt my eyes. I turned on my side, pulled the hood up on my jacket and tried to sleep. It was impossible. The night seemed to go on forever until eventually I could see the early light of dawn appear through the prison bars.

A naked Indian guy with a long, black beard and wearing a bright orange turban ran past me, waving his arms about in the air screaming, "I HAVE GOD POWER." I looked on confused. This was my first day. Was that going to be me? Life had begun to take its toll on me. Where was it all heading?

What was the meaning of life? These were questions that don't seem to have answers.

Some people are born lucky, some people fight for what they have, while others are just lost or trapped in limbo. Me? Well, I have no one to blame for who I am. I am who I am through the choices I made, making acceptance of my current predicament easy for me.

11

Chiang Mai Central Prison

PROZAC JACK WAS the only other Brit in Chiang Mai Central Prison (CCP). He chain-smoked Marlboro menthol cigarettes and was chronically depressed. Jack had lived in Thailand for more than ten years, but was hopeless at speaking Thai. He was tall, skinny and completely bald, and held his head low as if in shame.

"Bill, I am an innocent man. I have been given four years for nothing. It's all lies, I tell you, rubbish, complete and utter rubbish," he said in disgust. "The prosecutor requested that I serve 99 years. Can you believe it? 99 years! The newspapers back in England claimed I was at the top of Interpol's most wanted list. Can you believe that? Wanted! I have never had so much as a parking ticket," said Jack, the anger clearly audible in his voice. "Bill, Joe was my friend; we had known each other for years. We smoked ya ba together. I never held him captive or against his will. It's all lies. I am not a Gary Glitter, I'm not like that... pervert," he said, hurt and anger registering in his eyes.

Jack had been convicted of having sex with a fourteen-year-old hill tribe boy whom he knew as Joe. The police claimed he kept the boy locked in his room for two years as his sex slave. "I have been waiting eighteen months for the appeals court to hear my case. It's a scandal. They know I'm not guilty. It's face, Bill, they don't want to lose face. I'm not a fucking paedophile," Jack stated.

I had been inside this prison for a couple of days and all that time had heard Jack scream and shout relentlessly about his innocence. Jack was taking me to the visiting room. Christian missionaries visited the dozen or so foreign prisoners twice a week.

"Is there anyone I can contact for you?" asked the middle-aged woman behind the thick glass. The vent made her voice sound tinny. She had short, curly, mousy hair and a kind smile that lit up her face.

"Do you have family? I am sure they are worried about you." Her small voice oozed warmth. She was from New Zealand and her name was Kathleen. Her soft, blue eyes stared at me from behind the thick glass. I had no one I could contact. Addresses and phone numbers were lost.

"No, I'm alone, but thanks anyway," I said, quietly sad at the admission.

"But you do have someone. You have Jesus. And he loves you, Billy. Did you know that? Jesus loves you so much and so do I," said Kathleen.

"Err yeah, thanks," I said, feeling uncomfortable under her intent gaze.

"Would you like me to say a prayer for you?" said Kathleen as she placed her palms together and lowered her head closer to the vent. "Jesus, please watch over Billy. He is lost and needs you to help guide him. You are his shepherd, please show him the way to your heart…"

I looked over at Jack who mouthed the words "happy clappers" and raised his eyebrows to the ceiling. Kathleen finished her prayer and spoke about herself, her mission and how she helped the foreign prisoners in Thailand. She had paid for and left each of the foreigners some noodles, bread and fruit.

"Are you religious, Bill?" Jack asked me on the walk back to the foreigner section.

"No, not really, I don't go to church or anything like that," I told him honestly.

"I'm a Jew, but don't tell Dr Death," said Jack pointing at a very old German prisoner.

"Dr Death? Why do they call him that?" I asked curiously.

"Helfred is wanted in about a dozen different countries. He's a conman. He claims he's discovered a cure for cancer. A little bird told me that he's a mass murderer. Absolute animal if you ask me, stealing off the sick; what kind of man is that?" said Jack, puffing frantically on his cigarette. "I don't bother with anyone in here, Bill, and I suggest you do the same," he said, walking quickly and slapping away at the mass of outstretched arms begging him for cigarettes. I had worked Jack out; he was in denial about his own sexuality.

I looked around CCP, the monkey house of northern Thailand. It was a small complex with a huge population of over four thousand inmates. In every area of the prison people were either sleeping, eating, singing, sucking or fucking. The open-air toilets we had to use stank to high heaven. The smell of piss was so strong it would assault your nostrils. The burning feeling at the back of the throat and a constant bad taste in your mouth made it sometimes feel like you were breathing toxic acid.

On weekends the ladyboys would set up bungalows – little makeshift tents made out of old smelly blankets – and prostitute themselves for as little as four packets of cheap cigarettes.

"Hey, farang, you like fuck arse me?" shouted a ladyboy outside the toilet I was using. He lifted up his top to show me a perfect pair of tits that could have easily been mistaken for the real thing. "You like?" he said, squeezing them tightly and pouting seductively. If a guy in a thong and lipstick did it for me, then I would be the luckiest man in here, I thought.

But instead I decided I'd leave that for Jack.

"I don't do men, but if I did I'd do you," I joked.

"I is a lady, not man," he shrieked. You have to be careful about upsetting these ladyboys. They can get unpleasant, and the last thing you want is to find yourself in a fight with a crazy, mixed-up guy with female hormones.

"Yes, you're a woman. You're a beautiful woman. In fact you look like a Rolls-Royce in a scrap yard," I lied and showed him my most charming smile. He calmed down, smiled and blew me a kiss.

"You no like ladyboy?" said a young Thai man, pissing in the cubicle next to me. He was staring at my penis, watching me urinate.

"You want same me?" he said, shaking his huge penis. It looked like a blown up rubber glove.

"What the fuck have you done to your cock? It's a mess," I said, disgusted at what he was showing me.

"Operation, friend me do," he said, smiling and obviously proud of his friend's handiwork. "You want me do for you? Many lady like. Jing, jing," he said, eager to please.

"You must be joking. It looks like a dead squid. Why's it so fat?" I asked, getting ready to leave the toilets.

"Is Vaseline, inject inside, make big. Have ball bearing, friend me sew inside, make sex good. Ladyboy many happy," he said, winking.

I walked away, shaking my head in disbelief. I would hate to see what that would do to someone's arsehole.

The days were long and hot. The food was either chicken-head soup with sticky rice or lumps of pork fat. I lived on noodles, eating them dry. Jack constantly walked to and fro, smoking his cigarettes. The other foreigners sat around playing chess or sleeping on straw mats. There were a few foreigners who I didn't like – a couple of Australians and an Iranian who walked around like they owned the joint. I just sat alone and observed my surroundings.

We spent most of our time in "Den Piset" the induction centre, a huge building block that was old and crumbling. It housed all the newcomers and a handful of foreigners. We were kept away from the main population. We got to see all the new prisoners, mostly young boys. Jack would often sit with them, plying them with cigarettes and sweets from the shop. Horses for courses, I thought.

The only other foreigner missing from the induction centre was a crazy old Indian guy called Singh. He lived amongst the Thais, the only people who would accept him. The trusties, known as "blueshirts", were told to keep him out of Den Piset because he was trouble and apparently violent and disliked by the rest of the foreigners. I couldn't wait to meet him, and it wasn't long before it happened.

I actually heard him before I saw him. It was the most terrible sound I had ever heard, coming through the speakers. It sounded like a massacre.

"That's singing Singh," said Jack. "Every weekend he gets up on the stage and sings shitty Indian songs."

The prison had a band that was allowed to perform live at the weekends. They had all the right equipment – electric guitars, huge speakers and a stage set up in "Sala Deng", the control section. The guards let Singh sing his Indian songs. The crowd booed. He wasn't popular but he didn't care.

One weekend, Singh stopped me as I was heading towards the toilets. "Hello, my friend. You are new, are you not? I have seen you around. You stay alone I see, that is good. Come sit down, this is my home," he said, patting a place on the floor close to the toilets.

"You are from England, yes? Don't trust the Australian and Iranian doggers," Singh warned. "These people are not so good people. And Jack, he likes to fuck the little boys. What sort of man is this? Thailand have many beautiful lady, yes? Why he want to fuck little boys?" spat Singh in disgust. "They're all doggers! But you, you are different, yes? Yes, I can see, I know these things, my God tells me. I have God power," said Singh, punching the air with his clenched fist, obviously insane.

He wore a bright orange turban and had a long, scraggly black beard with bits of food in it. "You like my singing? I dance very good too." Singh jumped up and performed a little jig and began singing terribly, causing a small group of sleeping Thais to complain. "Fuck you, doggers! This is my home, you stinking animals," he growled. "Don't be minding these filthy peasants. I watch them every day. They shit and wipe their arse with their hand, then eat the food, same dog," he said.

It was eighty-four days before I was charged with handling stolen goods. I pleaded guilty and was sentenced to three years; I was lucky. The weapons were not mentioned; in fact I believe they were stolen by the arresting officers. They were welcome to them. I just wanted to get out the easy way, only I don't do things easy.

I did my time hard.

Every fucking day of it was a war.

12

Chiang Mai Surprise

I HAVE ALWAYS been a rebel without a cause, always defended the underdog, and always fought other people's battles. In this case I was helping Aldo, a fat, old Italian and his American buddy, John. Both of these guys were getting bullied by two Australians and an Iranian.

I had only been in the prison for a couple of months and had watched these three cowards physically and verbally abuse the two old men. It had to stop. I couldn't allow this to continue if it could be helped. Actually, the two old guys made good targets. They were forever complaining about conditions and the human rights they were convinced applied to them. They were dead wrong.

I approached the cowards who were responsible for the escalating physical and verbal abuse, and asked them to lay off and give the old guys a break. We were all foreigners and should stick together.

I was standing by my cell when Ali the Iranian came walking towards me, screaming: "Hey, motherfucker!

Who are you?" He was up in my face and my back was against the wall. The two Australians, John and Daniel, were standing either side of him, and I could see a small wooden chair in John's left hand and a look of pure hatred in his eyes. I really didn't want to fight. I clenched both my fists, readying myself for what seemed to be the inevitable. I wasn't scared; these were not thoughts I entertained.

I looked towards Daniel and could see big nasty metal rings on both his hands, the cheap ones the Thais made to sell at the weekends.

"Motherfucker!" Ali continued to scream. I said nothing. I was cornered. Ali threw a punch but, before it connected, I launched myself at him. Ali was over six feet tall, wiry and strong-looking. I had to act fast. I was sinking my teeth deep into his neck when something solid hit me on the back of the head. Out of the corner of my eye I could see John swinging the chair. I sank my teeth deeper into Ali's neck, tasting his blood. Daniel smashed his ringed fist into my face. I could hear Ali's blood-curdling screams. He was pleading and begging for me to let go. I was growling like a rabid dog holding a bone.

A whistle blew in the distance and I could hear the sound of footsteps running towards us. Hands grabbed me around the neck. "Stop, farang!" I was being pulled off Ali, who quickly ran off screaming: "Motherfucker! You die!"

Ali ran down the landing holding his neck, his blood seeping through his fingers. John and Daniel stared back at me, eyes wide open, with a look of horror on their faces. Blood was everywhere – on my clothes, my face and particularly around my mouth. I grinned back at them with blood-stained teeth, raised my middle finger and screamed, "Shit bags! Three onto one!" I had a gash above my right eye; my white T-shirt looked as though it was painted red with both my own and Ali's blood. The trusty took one look at me and marched me to the medic's office to be looked at by one of the medical trusties.

Once inside the medic's office I heard laughing. The Thais were laughing and talking about me but I couldn't understand what was being said. They were pointing at me and could see the look of confusion on my face.

"What?" I shouted angrily.

"Hey, farang! You no good boxer!" they mocked me. Anger surged through my body. I was enraged. I jumped up from where I was seated and smashed my fist into the jaw of the nearest trusty, knocking him down. Immediately I was pounced on by a number of Thai inmates. I heard the whistle being blown again for the second time that morning.

While I was pinned to the floor the guy who I had attacked was back up and smashing his foot into my already bloody face. I couldn't move. Somebody else had me in a stranglehold with a baton while his knee was pressed into my lower back. My breathing became laboured and I heard shouts of "Let go!" before I lost consciousness.

As I came around, dazed and confused, I could feel myself being dragged along the floor by my legs. There were two guards walking either side of me, swinging their wooden batons. My head was throbbing and my throat felt raw. Being pulled along like a rag doll made me feel weak and helpless. The next thing I could remember was being dragged down a flight of dirty concrete stairs, my head connecting with a heavy thud on each step.

I lost consciousness once again and welcomed it.

I awoke in the compound of the control section, flat on my back with the midday sun beating down relentlessly on my face. Flies were hovering around my head and there were huge red ants crawling all over my body and biting me – pure agony. I tried to raise my hand to swipe away the ants; it felt like a dead weight. I groaned out loud as pain wracked my body. I desperately needed water.

I opened my eyes slowly and heard movement close by. There was a silhouette of a person heading towards me. My eyesight was a little hazy and it was difficult to focus. "Help me!" I groaned, my voice rasping.

My face was being dabbed with cool water as my vision became clearer. I could see what appeared to be a young girl in her early twenties wearing bright red lipstick and a short pageboy hair cut. She smiled at me. "You OK?"

She was a he.

His voice, which sounded like Minnie Mouse on helium gas, gave him away despite his beauty and winning smile. It always amazed me how feminine and delicate some of these ladyboys looked.

"Your face look no good. Me name Jom. I help you". Jom dabbed at my face with a piece of tissue and cleaned off the now dry, crusted blood. He was gentle and showed me kindness. He told me he and three other transsexuals had to stay inside the compound for their own protection. These were the only ladyboys in the prison who had had the full operation to change their gender and now possessed all the beauties of a real woman. "I have pussy," Jom told me proudly. "If I go outside compound, danger – four thousand man want boom boom me."

Jom finished cleaning my face then left to go to the commander's office. I managed to sit up. My face was swollen and, as I touched it, I could feel the lumps and bumps. My eyes began to well up with tears. I felt defeated, lost, totally alienated and alone again. I suddenly became angry with myself for having these feelings. The tears stung my eyes and I blinked to allow them to run down my cheeks.

Jom returned five minutes later with news: the building chief wished to speak to me. Jom was only small but he managed to help me onto my feet. I felt dizzy once up but held onto Jom's shoulder as he helped me to walk to the commander's office. "I translate for you, OK?" I just nodded and followed him into the cool, air-conditioned room where I was ordered to sit on the floor.

The building chief, an overweight man in his early fifties with a grey moustache and a serious look on his face, was speaking to Jom in rapid Thai. Jom looked at me, then back to the building chief.

"What's he saying?" I asked.

"He say you no good farang. Fighting very bad," Jom replied

"And?" I asked, knowing there was more.

"You have to move out of foreigner section, stay with Thai people," he told me.

"What! They'll kill me out there."

The second-in-command spoke up: "My name Prisit. You like fighting, then maybe you can join the boxing team," he suggested. Prisit was a good-looking man with a kind face; he was tall and smartly dressed in his brown uniform. "Nobody will hurt you, I promise," he assured me. He then winked at me, "OK, William, you can go now, but please, if you fight, fight in the ring." He held out his hand. "Gentleman hand shake, OK, Western style." I shook his hand and immediately knew I could trust Prisit. I then bowed slightly, out of respect to the building chief, and left the office.

Jom followed me outside, clapping his hands together excitedly, and said, "You lucky, farang. Prisit very good man. He like you." Jom said that I wasn't being punished but I would have to spend a month in the compound until everything calmed down.

13

Boxing Team

THE PRISON BOXING team trained hard, very hard. Every time I tried to enter the gym I was told to go away. "You no welcome," said a tired, old-looking Thai trainer who called himself the Black Superman. Whenever I approached he would rush over to lock the gate and block my entrance. I just stood outside and stared through the fence, watching the guys sparring.

I pleaded with them to allow me to train. I couldn't understand why they were so reluctant to let me box, or even work out. It had to be because I was a foreigner.

"Hey, let me in," I shouted, but the blank faces that stared back told me the answer was going to be no. "Hey, Ajarn," I shouted. The ajarn, or teacher, was the guy I needed to speak to. In Thailand ajarns are respected.

This time I got his attention; he walked towards me coughing and then spat, "Ari farang yah ma yung gap pom, na." He spoke in machine-gun Thai. I understood what it meant – don't bother me, foreigner. I had heard it every day for three weeks.

When I showed him a carton of Krung Thip cigarettes a huge smile magically materialized on his face. "Let me train and they're yours." The gate opened.

"Welcome, my friend me," he said in broken English as I walked past him. I headed over to the ring and chose a pair of battered red bag gloves. All the equipment was old and of poor quality, but it was a gym, the blood-and-sweat type. This was my turf!

I pounded the heavy bag for 30 minutes and the ajarn watched me. All the while he smoked. He was a tall man, in his late forties with an air of authority and kind brown eyes. Neither of us spoke. He just smiled and gave me the thumbs-up. Each morning I went to the gym and the gate was now left open for me.

Boxing every day kept me busy and allowed me to forget the austere surroundings of the prison, if only for a while. The ajarn's name was Chamnan, but he insisted I call him Nan. We became very close friends. He invited me to break bread with him and a few of the other boxers. Thais are generous with food, and would always offer what they had. Some were lucky enough to have families who prepared food for them and passed it in during visits. Outside in the gym compound, huge meals were laid out on a mat. Five-star fried chicken with sweet sauce, fish, beef, vegetables and a variety of red and green curries, all served with soft boiled rice. This was a joy to the heart, but a much bigger delight to my stomach.

My prison ID.

Working on the set of Rambo.

I briefly met Sylvester Stallone on the set of Rambo.
I found Stallone to be a total gentleman. He's also a fine actor.

This picture takes me back to
a happier time in my youth.

You can get out of shape
very quickly in prison.

Organised crime gangs control Thai prisons.
Among them the Samurai.

My first Muay Thai fight. Nimdam and Papa
are seen watching in the background.

Nan and the Ching Mai boxing team.

Nan told me that he had been a soldier in the Royal Thai Army before he came to prison. On guard duty one night two drunken police officers stumbled towards him, waving their firearms about in an aggressive manner. They grabbed hold of Nan and screamed, "We are police!" Fearing for his life, he pulled out his side arm and shot them both dead. He was 21 years old, now he was 47. I liked Nan. He treated me with respect and he told the other boxers to treat me the same way.

Songkran, the Thai New Year, was coming up. The whole country went crazy during this holiday, celebrating with huge water fights and parties that lasted at least a week. The prison would hold their own parties with live music, plenty of singing and a boxing competition. Nan asked me to box – not Muay Thai, just plain old boxing. I was to fight Pon, his best boxer. I had a slight bump on my left side, Nan questioned me and I told him about the accident I had the year before in Laos. I was the first foreigner ever to box in the prison. Nan helped me get ready and said he would be in my corner.

Pon was strong and very fast, with a lot of experience. We both weighed 75kg. Pon disliked foreigners and would make it known. "Farang kwai," (buffalo) Pon spat with venom. This is the lowest insult in the Thai language. It means that you are just a stupid, dumb animal.

The day of the fight arrived, the weather was muggy and the temperature high, into the 30s. Pon was already waiting when I stepped into the ring. A huge crowd had gathered to watch the fight. Nan massaged my arms and shoulders in readiness. The announcer introduced us both to the crowd. The crowd cheered to give us a warm welcome. We touched gloves before the bell sounded.

I came out jabbing fast, but Pon was quick and parried my punches easily, countering with some of his own. In boxing, footwork is essential and I used mine well, moving in quickly, bobbing and weaving from side to side, feigning a jab and coming over the top with a solid, right cross which connected with Pon's nose. Blood gushed from a cut on the bridge of his nose and spattered the already blood-stained canvas. Pon took the punch well, slipped to my left side and sent a huge left hook to my kidney. I dropped to one knee as pain engulfed me.

The ref began counting me out – one, two, three, four… I was back up by the count of eight. I wiped my sweat-drenched and bloody gloves on my vest and held my hands up high to show the ref I was capable of defending myself. To my relief the bell sounded, ending the first round.

In the corner, Nan looked concerned: "Billy, you OK?"

I breathed heavily. "Yeah, but my old injury's playing up I guess," I told him. I looked over at Pon, who stared and smiled at me in triumph as if the fight was over and he had already won.

"No look. Pon ladyboy," said Nan.

The bell sounded for the second round. I kept my guard up and my elbows tucked in tight to defend my body. Pon attacked me hard and fast again, connecting with solid punches on the side of my head. He was dancing round like a young Mohamed Ali, and every time I tried to counter with my own punches he was gone in another direction. If I was to have a chance I needed to cut him off, corner him.

Once I had him I unleashed a solid combination of uppercuts and hooks, but his guard held strong. He caught me again in my left side. This time I grabbed hold of him, afraid to let go, not wanting to go down again.

"Kwai!" Pon spat through his gum shield. I was breathing hard, my lungs gasping for air.

The ref got between us and broke the clinch. "Chok," (box) he shouted. It was difficult to box with Pon, he was a southpaw and led with his right, so I moved to my right, making it hard for him to pound me with his powerful left cross. Pon moved in quickly and fired off a right uppercut which jolted my head upwards, then smashed me in the body. The bell finished the round but Pon continued with his onslaught of body punches. The crowd booed.

I sat on my stool; ice-cold water was poured over my head and body. I was tired. Nan was speaking but I couldn't hear what he was saying. My left side hurt. Something didn't feel right. Nan slapped me around the face and said, "Billy, last round OK!" When I stood up the crowd were screaming my name.

"Nan, why are they screaming for me?" I asked confused.

"Pon, he no good man, people no like cheat."

The bell sounded for the final round. I came out, guard down in a showboating style, head poked forward, pulling faces to taunt Pon. He charged forward angrily, wide open. He threw a jab. I rolled under it and caught him under the chin with a beautiful left hook – knocking his gum shield out of his mouth – and then followed quickly with a solid right cross. Pon hit the canvas, the ref stopped the fight and sent me to a neutral corner and counted … eight, nine, ten.

Pon was out. The crowd cheered. Nan had a huge grin on his face as he helped me out of the ring. I winced in pain, my left flank throbbing. As Nan took me to see a medic, we passed Officer Prisit. "Very, very good, William," he cried and gave me the thumbs-up.

The medic recommended that the injury could not be treated at the prison and I was taken to an outside hospital in leg irons with two prison guards.

I couldn't believe it! My intestines had come through my abdominal wall and wrapped themselves around my muscle, according to the doctor at Marahat Hospital. It had been caused by my accident in Laos when I came off the rented motorbike.

"Billy, boxing now no good," said Nan when I returned to the prison. "Many danger. If you die me no happy." I could hear the concern in his voice, and see the hurt in his big brown eyes. "Fix OK, you box, me no problem," he shouted as I walked away.

I was determined to overcome this setback.

14

Tramadol and Transsexuals

AFTER A COUPLE of months in prison, I heard talk of a new foreign prisoner and his Thai girlfriend. They had been arrested for drugs. I knew it had to be Scott. I made my way over to the compound and watched as the new prisoners came in. There he was, the new foreigner. It was Scott and he looked a mess. He had lost so much weight he looked tired and gaunt and his dirty blonde hair was now long and hung loosely around his shoulders.

"Hey, Scott, over here. It's me, Billy," I shouted and waved my arms frantically to get his attention. He looked me straight in the eyes and at first didn't recognize me.

"Is that you, Bill? Shit, I was wondering where you went," he said and smiled.

"Scott, I'll come and see you tomorrow, OK?" I passed Nan a pack of cigarettes and a small bag of food to hand to him.

The following day, I made my way over to the foreigner section to greet Scott. He looked even worse than I expected. His hands were covered in horrible blisters, leaking puss, he smelt and his clothes were unwashed and torn. He held out his hand. I hesitated. "I ain't got Aids, Bill," he said, sounding hurt.

"Sorry, mate," I said, suddenly feeling ashamed. "But let's not shake just yet, hey, let your hands heal first. No offence," I said, hoping he understood my need for personal hygiene.

"Everybody's been nicked, Bill. You were lucky you only got caught with robbed gear. Three years? That's not a bad result. What do you reckon me and Joy will get?" he asked, hoping I was going to say a fine or something. To be honest, I didn't know and told him so.

"It could be from one year to twenty years. It's drugs, init? They're tough on all that over here."

You wouldn't believe what happened next. Scott hit the floor like a bag of spuds and started convulsing. Shit! I hoped I hadn't upset him and caused him to have a heart attack. The Thais just looked and pointed at Scott as he wobbled all over the place, laughing at the scene before them.

"Scott, are you OK, mate? What's wrong?" He had stopped shaking and was coming to. "Are you epileptic?" I handed him some water, not sure what his problem was.

"No, I've been taking loads of methadone. I feel really bad. Can you help me, Bill?" His eyes pleaded with mine. The only drugs available were a morphine-based painkiller called Tramadol. If you took enough of those they would keep the pain away. I had my own supply sent in by a Thai friend but needed them myself.

But the ladyboys could get anything. They sucked a lot of cock and business was good!

"Leave it with me. I'll speak to Noi. Just try not to do any more break dancing.

"These horrible scumbags don't care about their own people, so we mean nothing to them and don't you ever forget it. I'm telling you, if you lost a leg in here you'd only get a lousy paracetamol, and it wouldn't come cheap. If they see an opportunity to make a few baht out of you, they will, so don't show any weakness, stand tall and be a man amongst men," I said, hoping that he would learn fast and realise that this was no joke.

In prison your life depends on your ability to survive and show strength. I came from the streets of Liverpool so could deal with almost anything, but this place scared me and I knew it must have terrified poor Scott.

The biggest fear I had was falling in love with a fella, but Noi was one of the ugliest ladyboys I had ever seen. He had hobbit feet and hairy legs and every other word that came out of his mouth was an insult. He had a boyfriend who worked in the infirmary so he could get me the Tramadol.

"Aye, farang, ao arai? What you want, foreigner? You want me to smoke your cigar?" he said, licking his lips and doing an amazing imitation of sucking a penis. "Ooo, you like? I do for you free," he offered.

"No thanks, I'd rather suck my own cock. Can you get me some Tramadol?" I asked and handed him four packets of cigarettes.

"Sure, teerak, I get you taxi." The Thais called Tramadol taxis because they were coloured green and yellow, just like the local cabs.

As I sat and waited for Noi to return with the painkillers, another ladyboy came over to me and smiled at me. He had short, cropped hair and huge breasts inside a tight-fitting top.

"Hello, Billy, how are you?" I was surprised that he knew my name and it must have registered on my face, because he smiled again.

"You forget me, na. I May," he said, doing a twirl "Is me, you remember we smoke ya ba with your friend. Why you here? What you do wrong?"

I couldn't believe it was May. He looked so different with his hair short. The last time I had seen him it was long and he was wearing a dress and sported high heel shoes. Now he had a skinhead cut and was wearing green cotton shorts with a plain white T-shirt. On his feet were purple flip-flops that had seen better days.

"Yeah, of course I remember you, May. You just look different," I replied.

He smiled again, then waied me. "Is OK, mai bpen rai ka (never mind). I know, I fat now," he said patting his small stomach.

"No you're not fat, you look well," I said. He did look well; he had been in the prison for almost a year, had eaten regular meals and not used drugs. I explained to him what had happened to me and he told me that he felt sad that he had introduced me to the evils of ya ba. But I had a choice and I chose to take drugs no one forced me to use. The decisions were made by me and me alone.

"You so thin, pom mahk. Before you big like bear, you have to eat food many OK, na," said May, looking me up and down and shaking his head in sadness.

"It's OK, but you can't put weight on with the shitty food they give you here," I was forever hungry and was now living on sticky rice and Lactasoy milk. Noi returned and handed me a strip of Tramadol. I smiled at May, thanked Noi and left.

15

Big Trouble in Chiang Mai

DRUGS CAUSED A lot of problems for me. I had to buy my own medication and have it posted in. I could also buy medicines from Noi, at a higher price than the average Thai. They really thought we foreigners had money falling out of our arseholes, and the reality was we depended on family and charities abroad to help support us. I would always have problems with the medics who were inmates. Can you believe that? Inmates dispensed the drugs. They wanted to sell me my own medication. I was having none of that.

Scott was having a really bad time and had to be sent to an asylum for the criminally insane. He was prescribed huge amounts of lithium. His weight increased but most of the time he didn't even know where he was. That was the way some people coped, I guess.

I dealt with things totally differently. I began to find myself fighting a lot because of my pride. I hated being called an animal or a prick: "farang aye heeya, farang aye kway." My anger would get the better of me and I would fly into a rage, not caring how many people I fought, regardless of the pain I was in. Believe me, I often fought over five to one, and sometimes more than ten. I have had cuts above and below my eyes sewn back together with no anaesthetic. I have been beaten, battered, kicked and spat on and still I came back for more.

"Farang ba," crazy foreigner, they would call me. I was comfortable with being called that.

Years ago in British prisons, I would be called mad, nuts, lunatic and other names associated with psychopaths. This made me feel important, feared and respected. It sounds sad but being just Billy wasn't scary enough.

How do you punish a person? I thought, as I stood looking through the gates of Sala Deng.

I watched as a Thai inmate got beaten viciously by three commandos, their huge, heavy wooden bats directed towards vulnerable parts of his body. I saw his ankle take a solid whack. I could hear the force of the blow from where I stood. They then circled him slowly as he cowered in fear. When another commando smashed his bat onto the prisoner's knee caps, he howled in agony and writhed on the floor. Slowly, they circled him again, taking their time; the last commando suddenly brought his heavy bat down with a bone-crunching crack on the poor man's elbow. The guy yelled out so loud it echoed around the compound.

One of the guards kicked him in the face with his heavy boots, while he shouted at the inmate to be quiet. Blood poured down his face from a gash in his forehead. The Thai inmate curled up into a ball and held his head with both hands in an attempt to protect himself from the next volley of heavy blows. He was dragged into the office where the microphone had been left on, so the other inmates would be able to hear this guy sob and plead with the guards. His screams were broadcast over the speakers for a harrowing twenty minutes.

Later I found out from Nan that the trusties had found two ya ba pills in the seam of his shorts and wanted to know how he came into possession of these pills. The Thai prisoners will inform on you in an instant. They're cowards with no values or morals, who will simply point the finger to save their own skins. They can never be trusted.

As we were foreigners, the guards would never openly attack us, not wishing to attract negative attention from foreign embassies. However, they would use the trusties to do their dirty work.

A Japanese guy witnessed a brutal beating and drew a picture depicting what he had seen which he sent off to the Japanese embassy. This didn't go down too well with the guards. Shortly afterwards, the Japanese guy was on the floor having been attacked and badly beaten by a group of Thai inmates. The beating he took was brutal and required him to be rushed to hospital. He needed fifteen stitches along his nose. No one could prove anything but we all knew what had happened. The Thai prisoners love to gossip. To be honest I had no sympathy with him; it was his own fault; he constantly complained and had been warned many times to keep his nose out of Thai problems. Now he had had it smashed in and he looked like a Japanese Joe Bugner.

My problem with the prison infirmary began when they stopped giving me my painkillers.

"You pay," the trusty said to me while I was waiting at the medical hatch.

"Why should I pay? My friend sent me those pills," I told the trustee, wondering how this was going to turn out.

"You pay five packs of cigarette."

It was then I lost control of my anger. "Give me my fuckin' medication before I rip out your windpipe," I screamed, causing the medic to retreat in fear. Arms grabbed me from behind and two blueshirts manhandled me out of the infirmary. I pulled away, then felt a punch connect solid on the side of my jaw.

When I looked back I saw a big Thai man, stripped to the waist and covered in prison tattoos, laughing: "Go now, aye heeya."

The stairs were packed with people waiting to collect their medication. I smashed my fist into the tattooed man's chin, knocking him out cold on his feet.

The next thing that happened, the waiting cripples and junkies piled on top of me like a pack of dogs. Kicks and punches came from every direction. I was even attacked with a Zimmer frame by a guy who must have been in his eighties, his leathery old skin creased like a sucked prune.

My T-shirt was ripped off my back as I scrambled towards the stairs to escape their rage. A huge Cameroonian guy, Dildo, came charging up the stairs like a buffalo, slinging Thais out of his way. Dildo got between me and the mob and raised his hands high in surrender.

"Stop!" he roared at the angry pack. When he told me to run, I didn't need to be told twice. I dashed downstairs to safety.

It was the first time I can recall being saved by a black dildo.

This time I was in trouble; the trusty had lost a couple of teeth and had a broken arm. About a dozen witnesses claimed I had attacked him first. The building chief made the decision to punish me and had heavy chains welded onto my ankles – eight kilos of rusty metal.

"You no good man, kuhn ja bai chan ha," he said, sending me to the fifth floor. I was followed by four trusties, Nan being one of them.

"Billy, many danger, fifth floor. Jai yen yen, na," he said, warning me to have a cool heart.

16

The Fifth Floor

I WAS GREETED at the landing gate by a trusty wearing a huge smile. "Welcome, my friend, where you from?"

"Welcome to what?" I thought. I didn't want to be here. This was the only area in the prison that everyone feared. The shitlist, Chiang Mai's most dangerous: men serving thirty-five years plus, five cages, eighty prisoners in each. Cell number five held the death row inmates.

I was placed in cell number two with the only other foreigner up there – a paedophile serving thirty-five years. This beast was one sick, twisted twat! I'd heard about him from the other foreign prisoners. Hate consumed me. I wanted to rip his skeleton out of his arse and piss on his skin! This animal should have been in cell number five, ready for execution. To me he was nothing but a ghost.

Looking around the dark, gloomy cell, I could make out clothes hanging up on homemade lines, socks, underwear and even a ladies' bra. To me the cell resembled a Chinese laundry room. The smell was different up here too, a cocktail of shit, rotting flesh and human despair.

Everybody was made to wear shackles.

I found a small space in the middle of the room amongst cardboard boxes full of sweaty clothes, bits of rubbish and bottles of murky water of unknown origin that was definitely not Perrier or even drinkable by the look of it. The cell was full and looked like a container full of refugees with their belongings scattered everywhere. How could I stay here? My mind was working overtime. I needed to get out of here, but how? Suicidal thoughts rushed through my mind, but were quickly dismissed as insane.

Officer Prisit was my only hope. He liked me and called me the Oscar De La Hoya of Chiang Mai prison. Prisit suggested meditation as a way of relaxing. "Fighting no good. You have to be same like Buddha," he would often tell me. This time I knew he couldn't help me. It was out of his hands. I was being punished and I had to accept it before I drove myself crazy. I was told I would have to stay in this punishment cell in chains for one month.

Twenty-four hours in this inhuman hell hole was too long.

It was the same faces day in and day out that walked the narrow landing, spitting, snotting and breathing each other's oxygen. The feeling of being trapped was overwhelming, locked in this confined space with over 400 people. The pushing and shoving, the long queues for the toilet, the water shortages, all this was more than a man could stand. These inhumane conditions breached every human rights convention ever written, but here you could not seek any refuge in human rights.

To entertain themselves, the Thais would play card games all night, even though it was illegal. The cards were made out of milk cartons. Games such as high/low were a favourite. The prisoners would gamble everything they possessed. I learnt that they would bet on just about anything, even down to who would die next in the HIV ward of the prison infirmary. These maximum security cells had 24-hour surveillance and the only blind spot was next to the toilet, close to where I slept.

I found sleep impossible with the constant noise of the chains grating against each other. It was torture. We had to sleep, shower, shit, piss, eat and wash our clothes all in this one cell. I hated it and slipped into a deep depression. I made the decision to kill myself. I was going to hang myself from the bars in the corner of the cell and asked a young Thai guy called Lek to help me.

"Cannot help, Pi Billy. Officer no like people kill themselves. Against rule," he told me.

"What? There's a rule to say you can't kill yourself?" I said, disbelievingly.

"Yes, Pi Billy, very, very number-one no good," he said shaking his head sadly. "You die they beat us and punish you, kao jai?"

I didn't want anybody to be punished for my selfishness. "OK, I understand. Big mistake if you die!"

Days, weeks and even months passed by. I was forgotten, lost in the system. I had become one of them. I learned the language and the madness became normal.

"William! William Moore!" Somebody shouted my name. I looked up from my place on the floor to see a guard through the gated door. "Yes sir," I answered.

"William, you go hospital."

It was early, maybe 5.00am. I could hear the sounds of people moving about, loud coughing, the toilet flushing, and the rattle of chains.

"William!" He called out again. I struggled to my feet and made my way over to the gate that he was already unlocking. I stepped over the prone sleeping bodies of other inmates, careful not to stand on anyone. The sports socks Nan had given me helped protect me from any cuts caused by the shackles. I had tied a piece of string through the centre of the chain link to stop it from dragging along the floor. I put on my sandals and followed the guard slowly, the length of the chain restricting my normal pace.

We left the prison and headed to Marahat Hospital. My operation was scheduled for the next day and I was taken to a small ward on the seventh floor. It was clean and smelt fresh, the staff were polite and made me feel welcome. It felt good to be out of the prison.

The guard assigned to watch me was a lazy slob. He wrote down his phone number and handed it to me.

"You have problem, give nurse," he said, and then as an afterthought he added, "You run, you die, na!" He stuck his finger to his head and pulled an imaginary trigger, then smiled at me and left.

I lay back on the big comfy bed and smiled. This was the first time I had been in a bed for almost a year and I was going to make the most of it. I felt almost human again. Only the heavy chains which remained on at all times separated me from the other patients. The nurses had given me a sarong to help hide them. The food was much better than the prison muck, but it was still a bland diet of rice soup with small pieces of meat.

The following day, after surgery, I woke up back in my ward. Kathleen, the missionary, was sitting beside my bed and holding my hand, squeezing it gently. "Hey, how are you feeling?" she asked, smiling warmly.

"OK," I winked and managed a smile. She had been sitting next to my bed all the while, waiting for me to come round. She was an amazing woman and dedicated to her mission. She helped everybody she came to see at the prison, and really loved her work. We chatted for a short while, and then she told me she had spoken to the surgeon who said the operation had gone well. I had a drain attached to my stomach to release any excess blood or fluid, and this would probably be there for the next five days.

"Hey, that's great! I mean, you won't have to stay in that filthy prison," she said, leaning forward and kissing me softly on the cheek. "Now what would you like me to bring you to eat?" she asked me.

"I want everything! KFC, pizza, McDonald's. Oh yeah, don't forget the fries," I said, smiling.

"We'll see, OK," she said, laughing. "Here's some money to help buy food and drinks." She left, but came back to see me each afternoon.

After a few days I was feeling much stronger. I had the drain removed and the doctor said he would allow me to stay a couple of days longer.

The prison guard did his rounds once a day, usually at about 8.30 in the morning so I had freedom to wander around the ward. But I soon got bored.

The fire exit was situated a couple of yards away from my ward. One day, I walked a little further than usual and headed down the exit stairs, my shackles safely hidden under the sarong. On reaching the ground floor, my heart racing fast in my chest, I looked behind me and back up the stairs, nervous that someone may have noticed me missing. All was quiet; nobody had raised the alarm. Feeling more confident, I headed towards an open door.

Outside, there were people seated on mats eating food. I could see shops on the other side of the chain-link fence and the one that interested me the most was a pharmacy. I still had the money Kathleen had given me and no one paid me any attention as I walked the short distance out of the hospital gates towards the drugstore.

"Hello, sir, may I help you?" The pretty, young assistant behind the counter asked me.

"Yeah, give me those," I said, pointing at a box of Tramadol painkillers. She took my money, showing no interest in my dishevelled appearance.

Back on the street, I walked slowly towards the 7-Eleven. Escape was almost impossible, but right now I would be classed as unlawfully-at-large, and could be shot on sight. FUCK IT, I wasn't going back until I had bought a pack of cigarettes. Pleased with my purchases, I quickly made my way back to the hospital. The fire exit door was still open. Again nobody paid me any attention and I was soon back in my ward undetected.

When the painkillers and cigarettes were almost gone, I began to have serious thoughts of escape. The guard was seldom around, which gave me plenty of time to make a break for it, but I needed to remove the shackles if a serious attempt was to be made.

The night before I was due to return back to the prison I made the decision to flee the hospital.

I climbed out of the bed silently and slipped down the back stairs. Outside the hospital it was quiet, the streets were empty. I was sweating profusely. My adrenalin was pumping as I climbed over the small chain-link fence with ease. Stealing a car was my only plan. I walked for what seemed like miles. It was almost 3.00am when I thought, this is crazy! How far did I think I was going to get? I couldn't remove the heavy shackles and was pretty sure nobody would be willing to help me. It was hopeless, an impossible task that was destined to fail, ending in either further imprisonment or death. I hurried back to the hospital and my ward as fast as the shackles allowed me to. With a heavy heart, I knew I had to go back and serve the rest of my sentence.

It was my only choice.

I moved into Nan's cell. He and Prisit compromised and allowed me to move into Hong Nak Geela, the sports room. There were sixty-eight inmates in this cell by my last count. I had by this time secured myself a good bed and enjoyed eating decent food. After only six weeks of resting, I begged Nan to allow me to train. I needed to be active.

"No, cannot, nong chai, an tarai, very danger," he said. He meant well and it warmed my heart that he cared. However, I hated being stagnant and would watch with envy as the other guys in my cell trained for hours, kicking and punching the heavy bags.

I lied and told him I was well and ready to train. I didn't think I was going to come out of Thailand alive and I wanted to go down fighting. He was reluctant and said no, but I didn't listen. The operation wasn't a success; it was a botched job. My condition was now becoming worse. So what choice did I have? I could either sit around in the baking heat, getting depressed, using drugs and becoming brain dead or die with fire in my heart.

When the gloves were on I was free from the pain. It didn't exist. I was lost in my own head and took a journey to places I once enjoyed. The Thais thought I was mad. They had never come across someone as stubborn as me. I would punish myself and train in the scorching heat until I collapsed, then I would pick myself up and carry on even harder. Fear had long since left my soul. Maybe I thought there was nothing to live for, or maybe being around so much death had conditioned me to accept it.

There was a guy I slept next to called Yow, a kind-hearted soul who always smiled no matter what life threw at him. He was serving thirty-seven years for five hundred ya ba pills. We were the same age. He had fought in Muay Thai competitions since the age of five. We would train together and I would teach him English. He had a twelve-year-old daughter called Ning whom he loved dearly. His behaviour in the prison was good, so he was allowed to have a once-a-year open visit and was excited at the thought of holding his daughter in his arms once again. The day before his visit with his lovely daughter, Yow died. I woke up to find him dead next to me, stiff as a board. They said it was TB but we all knew it was HIV. I cried for him and his daughter.

This is how I lived, watching people around me die.

Scott kept himself busy by getting tattoos all over his body. They looked really good. "Why don't you get one done, Bill. You won't get it cheaper anywhere else," he said, while wincing in pain as the small Thai guy called Toom jabbed at his back with the bamboo stick.

"You're joking, aren't you? You don't know where those needles have been," I said, looking at the half-naked Scott, who was high on cough pills known as "yellow motorbike," a drug that causes you to hallucinate when taken in large quantities.

"They don't use needles, Bill, they use guitar strings and they're new. I've got some spare ones. Toom here can do you a good tattoo. Isn't that right, Toom? My friend me tattoo, you do, OK?" said Scott in pidgin English to the nodding Toom, who probably didn't understand a word Scott said.

I thought about it and decided I would get one. I wanted a picture of a Muay Thai boxer. It took a week of being stabbed in the back with guitar strings tied to a piece of bamboo, the result a huge boxer performing the ram muay. Nan was impressed. I thought it looked shit and was disappointed, especially with the pink writing he used when he ran out of my chosen colours.

When I went back to the hospital for a check-up, the doctor was, or at least pretended to be, concerned. He decided I needed further surgery. I didn't object. It was all time out of the prison for me and access to more painkillers to dull the misery and forget my surroundings.

I had gone past caring a long time ago and decide to allow the Thai government to own and use my body.

17

A Guest at the "Bangkok Hilton"

WHEN I WOKE up in the hallway of Nakhon Ping hospital, I was dazed and groggy after the operation to re-repair my hernia. The anaesthetic was wearing off and I knew it wouldn't be long before I started to feel the pain. I tried to move my legs but the chains bit into my ankles. The duty officer in charge of watching me was not around. They never were. And I needed the toilet. I couldn't move freely this time. The guard had chained the shackles to the metal frame of the bed with a heavy-duty padlock. So I shouted to a nurse. People stopped and stared, then smiled and moved on. I felt helpless; I needed to empty my bladder and felt the warm urine run down my leg. I couldn't help myself and didn't feel any shame.

I must have drifted off back to sleep. I felt someone shove me and heard, "Wake up! Wake up, we go now." As I struggled to open my eyes, a sudden pain shot through my side and I saw a guard, the one called Fierce. He was the biggest Thai I had ever seen. He was huge, stood over six-foot four and must have easily weighed twenty stone.

"We go now," he said

"Go where?"

"Prison Bangkok," Fierce replied with a smile that said in no uncertain terms that he was thrilled to see me suffer.

The clock at the far end of the hallway said 5.30am. Bangkok was over 1,000km away – at least a fifteen-hour journey from Chiang Mai by bus. How long had I been in hospital? Eighteen or nineteen hours, maybe. There was a drain in my abdomen and I still felt weak. I must have misheard Fierce; they couldn't possibly expect me to travel in this condition.

"Quick, we go now. Bus for you wait," he said while unlocking the padlock.

"I'm sick, cannot go," I screamed, but they weren't listening. They pulled me off the bed. Fierce stood by the exit, holding his shot gun. "Get your hands off me, I can walk myself," I said, snarling at the guard who pulled on my arm. He let go. I inched my way forward towards the door. "Where are my flip-flops?" I asked.

"Flip-flops? No understand."

"Rong tao, shoes, sandals, flip-flops. Kao jai?"

"No have," replied Fierce. The shackles were scraping against my bare skin. I walked slowly, holding the drainage bottle in my right hand. The bus was waiting outside the hospital entrance. I couldn't believe what I was seeing; it was full to the rafters with prisoners.

I searched the row of blank faces that stared down at me. I knew them, it was the boxing team. I could see my friend Nan. "Hey, nong chai, sabai dee mai?"(You OK, little brother?) he shouted down to me through the mesh-covered windows. "We go Phitsanulok, boxing."

OK, I get it. That's why there were so many people on the bus. The boxing and football teams were being dropped off at their annual sports event at Phitsanulok prison, while I would go on to Bangkok.

Nan made room for me to sit down and rest

"Thailand no good, nong chai," he said but I was in terrible pain and could only nod. His eyes held sympathy, mine welled up with tears and I quickly turned away, embarrassed and ashamed for displaying emotions in this inhuman environment.

"Jai yen yen," Nan said as he placed a comforting hand on my shoulder.

The bus was crammed with Thais, but there were also other foreigners, at least seven of them. Scott was there as was my Indian friend, Slim Khan. Slowly they made their way over to me through the crowded bus; people were jammed in, squashed like cattle.

"Billy, my friend, how is your pain feeling? These people in the prison are very no good. But not to worry, our tenancy on this god-awful bus won't be long, I am suspecting now. Maybe four hours many people will be kindly departing," gushed Slim.

Scott was stoned as he had taken a handful of yellow motorbikes before getting on the bus. Now his pupils were hugely dilated and he was hallucinating. "I'm wasted, Bill. I feel like the Lawnmower Man."

I sat back with my head against the window and closed my eyes, the pain throbbing in my side and the bottle held securely in my hand. "Nong chai, cigarette?" Nan said as he handed me an unopened pack of Krung Thip. Gratefully I took them and lit one up, inhaling the smoke deep into my lungs. "Lard Yao, no same Chiang Mai. Chiang Mai cheap cheap, you fight you die," warned Nan, and I believed what he said. Lard Yao was a place to be feared.

"You filthy dingo," Bill the old Australian shouted at one of the young Thai boxers who was taking a dump into a plastic bag next to where he sat. Everybody laughed at Bill. He was a miserable old sod at the best of times. He was an old Vietnam War vet and a crazy old coot. He had his lips to the small window and was breathing hard. "Goddamn filthy animals, shittin' in bins. Strewth, that stinks," he moaned.

Finally we arrived at Phitsanulok and it was time to say good bye to my dear friend Nan. He handed me a couple of packets of cigarettes. "Forget me not, nong chai," he said as he grabbed my hand and wished me luck. We smiled at each other, then he left the bus and was gone.

I was going to miss him.

Twelve of us remained on the bus. Four Thais were to be executed at Bang Kwang prison, one was headed for Bombat and the rest of us were going to Lard Yao, which was part of the notorious Klong Prem jail, known ironically as the "Bangkok Hilton".

We reached the gates of the prison late. It was almost 9.30pm and it was a daunting feeling to look up at those massive gates and imagine the hell that lay beyond them.

Once inside the gates of the main section, we were quickly rushed to building number six. We passed through five huge gates. Shit, this place was huge! The tower out front reminded me of an old airport control tower and I could see gun turrets on each corner of the walls. Walking was difficult and the pain had increased. My bare feet were bleeding. "I need to go to the hospital!" I told one of the guards who was escorting us to our destination.

"Now closed, tomorrow open," he said. I knew it was pointless as they weren't going to listen.

Upon entering my cell inside building six, I found it was a lot smaller than the ones in Chiang Mai, but still it held up to 40 people.

When the door slammed shut, all eyes looked up from their places on the floor and stared at me. I must have looked a terrible sight, standing there with my bottle of blood in my hand, still shackled.

It was obvious I was in pain. A big Thai guy jumped to his feet, looked around the room, and kicked a sleeping man nearby in the ribs.

"Bie!" (move) he ordered the man. "OK, farang, you sleep here." I sat down on the hard concrete floor, then lay down and tried to dream myself to be in any place other than here. I could only sleep a dreamless sleep; nothing could help me escape the dire situation I was in. I raged inside at my treatment or lack of it. I had been stripped of all my dignity. Every facet of my human rights had been violated and no one I cared about knew.

18

Welcome to Hell

PEOPLE DIED LOUDLY on the fifth floor in Klong Prem Hospital. The screams were horrendous and hopeless. All the beds were full. Dying wasn't easy to watch and the sick kept getting sicker. They knew they were on their way out. Their Aids-riddled bodies were in the final stages of organ failure. There was runaway sepsis, no pain relief; it was terrible.

Those who could still see could only watch as their dead and failing tissue was eaten alive. I had been in this ward for over a month, recovering from my operation, but I feared infections and wanted to leave. HIV, TB and flesh-eating diseases ran rife in the infirmary. The drain in my abdomen and surgical staples had been removed and the nurse signed the papers to have me sent back to Lard Yao.

Drugs were widely available in Lard Yao, corruption was endemic, and prison guards were lax and took huge bribes from the Thai gangs who wanted to stay in business. Heroin and crystal meth ("ice") were widely used. Every day was like Beirut. It made Chiang Mai prison look like a kindergarten.

Scott introduced me to Eliyas, a small Burmese guy with hawk-like features and greasy, black hair combed back with cheap gel. I instantly disliked him. He had a face you couldn't trust, and eyes that gave away his true intent.

"He looks like a slippery one, him," I said to Scott, judging the Burmese right there on the spot.

"He is, but if you need anything until the embassy comes up to see you, he can help you," Scott said quietly as Eliyas came strolling over with his hands tucked deep into his shorts.

"You need anything, you speak to me! You want to fly, you speak to me. Heroin, ice, Valium, you come see me. You cannot trust the Thai prisoners, but you can trust me, na," said Eliyas, with what sounded to me like his best sales pitch to the newcomers in the prison.

Eliyas could sell anything from sausage rolls to arse holes. He lived with a transvestite called Lena. Lena was ugly, Quasimodo-ugly, and in his forties. His only assets were his huge set of tits and his old arse. Eliyas fancied himself as a drug dealer, a pimp and a money lender and had a small shop which sold a variety of goods from food to cosmetics. He gave foreigners unlimited credit but at high interest rates and, unlike most of the shop owners, he was prepared to wait for his payment, at a price.

The hospital had refused to prescribe me any painkillers. I suffered deep burning pain and had a certain feeling that something was badly wrong. Eliyas would always be there, hovering around and touting for business. "Hey, my friend, you need money? I can help," he said, while waving a 1,000 baht note in my face.

"I don't need your money." Actually, I did as I was absolutely broke. However, I didn't want to slip into that never-ending circle of struggling to pay off debt after debt.

"But, Billy, you sick, yes? I can help take away the pain. Heroin is good medicine," he said, winking like it was a secret and rubbing his dirty hands through his greasy hair. I didn't want to get involved with using drugs in here. I had heard the stories of what had happened to people who were in debt.

"Look, Eliyas, I'm OK. Thanks but no thanks," I told him, fighting with my inner self to say no.

"No problem. If you need to fly, you know where I am," he said, still waving his money as he walked away.

"He's a scum bag, him," I said to Scott.

"He was like that with me when I first got here. I only buy biscuits from him and a bit of tobacco," said Scott.

"What do you think of it here, mate?" I asked, looking around amazed at the sheer size of the place.

"Hot!" he said while wiping the sweat from his brow onto his vest. "There's a British doctor, who comes here once a month. He only sees foreigners, and he gives you diazepam and Xanax. They knock you out. That's alright, init?" Drugs were constantly on Scott's mind, as they were on mine.

"Yeah, it is. When's he here next?"

"A couple of weeks, but you have to write a request to the White House."

"The White House! Who's going to read it, the president?" I answered in mock surprise.

"No," Scott laughed. "It's a building; the White House is the control section. You need to write a request for everything here and it has to be in Thai and English. And you've got to pay for the request paper, crazy hey? How was the hospital, Bill? Are you feeling any better?"

"No, mate, I'm in pain. It doesn't feel right," I said, holding my side where a huge swelling was visible.

"Was it bad up there?"

"It was hell! It stinks. There's a dead body every day. Cruel bastards, these Thais."

"It's good to have you back, Bill. It's been boring without you, nothing at all to do here but get your brain fried. The weather isn't like Chiang Mai, it's super-hot here."

"Yeah, thanks, mate. What's happening here then? Many foreigners?"

"Loads, about three hundred. There's a couple of Brits, not many, maybe four. Bill, we've got jam nek this week."

"What's jam nek?" I asked, confused.

"Jam nek? Oh yeah, they tell us what building we're going to. This is supposed to be the best building, Bill. You don't want to go to building three. That's where they send the nutters."

"And when's that?" I immediately asked, thinking I hope I don't go to building three. Being here in Lard

Yao was hell enough; I didn't want to be doing it with a load of lunatics.

"I'm not sure but he'll know," Scott said, pointing to a monster of a man with a huge, square head who was heading our way.

"Hey, buddy, how you doing?" said the monster, grabbing hold of Scott's outstretched hand and pumping it vigorously.

"I'm good, Sugar. This is my pal Bill," Scott said, introducing me to this Frankenstein of a man.

The guy didn't look like any Sugar I'd ever seen; he was huge, at least two metres tall and as wide as a barn. His shirt barely fitted his huge barrel of a chest and flabby stomach. "Hi, Bill," he said, "welcome to Shitsville."

"Tell him about jam nek, Sugar, he's just come back from the hospital."

Sugar filled me in on what I needed to know. He was a half-Thai, half-American in his early forties, charged with kidnapping and sentenced to eighteen years. They called him Sugar because he was a diabetic. Sugar lived on planet fantasy. He was full of shit. I liked him. He was funny without meaning to be and a constant source of entertainment. He was convinced the CIA was watching his every move. "Hey, Bill, do you know what they call me on the streets of Bangkok?" I didn't but big fat cunt sprang to mind.

"No, what's that then, Sugar?" I said, feigning interest.

"They call me the Punisher! I also go by the name of Samurai Sugar," he said seriously. I was dying to laugh, but didn't want to ruin his fantasy.

They moved five foreigners on the day of jam nek. I stayed in building six. Scott wasn't so lucky and was sent to building three to live with the nutters. This prison was huge, with nine buildings. Building six was the biggest and held over twelve hundred prisoners.

Without painkillers it wasn't long before I succumbed to the drug dealers of Lard Yao. The British doctor prescribed me diazepam and Xanax. These I sold to the Iranian gangs, who would sell them on to the Thais, who couldn't get access to these powerful drugs.

I too was in the grip of addiction within a few weeks of being here; it was my only escape.

"You want heroin, my friend? Is very good, make you fly high," said Hassan, smiling through gapped teeth and brushing his long brown hair out of his eyes. Hassan was known as a zig-zagger, a word that described a cheat, but not as bad as Eliyas. He had been in Klong Prem for nine years and spoke Thai fluently. "I can get good stuff, you want?"

My usual dealer Carlos, a Columbian, had been stabbed over a batch of bad merchandise. The heroin had me in its grip and I had no choice really but to trust the zig-zagger Hassan.

"Look, mate, who are you getting it from?" I asked, eyeing him up and down suspiciously.

"The Samurais, nobody have but them. I no cheat you, my friend, we share OK?"

The Samurais were a gang of HIV-infected junkies who had the heroin monopoly on lock-down. These were bad people who would kill you in an instant. Hassan knew them well.

"OK, but don't you dare cheat me. If you do I will drop you like a bag of spuds," I snarled.

"You crazy, my friend, why I cheat you?" Hassan said, his face creasing up in pain like I had just insulted his mother. "Go to the locker-room in twenty minutes." He took my money and went off to search for the Samurais and the heroin I needed.

Hassan pulled out a homemade syringe. "I make myself, is good yes?" said Hassan proudly.

"It's a biro! Where's the plunger?"

"No plunger, I suck and blow, we inject, is good."

"Are you mad? Just split the straw in half, I am not sticking that filthy thing in my body."

"OK, no problem, my friend, but please help me, I need you to watch the door," pleaded Hassan. I watched as Hassan mixed his half of the heroin with water. He then sucked the fluid from the small metal spoon.

"My friend, don't watch me, watch the door," hissed Hassan.

But I couldn't, I was transfixed by what he was doing. He found a vein and sucked through the pen to draw up the blood. Once he was satisfied, he blew hard, forcing the blood and the fluid back into his vein. His face visibly relaxed, his eyes became heavy. I could see he had left this prison. The walls for him had just melted away.

"OK, your turn to fly, my friend," he said, offering me the syringe. "Trust me, it's the only way in here," he said slurring his words.

I may be crazy, but I am not insane. I knew that amount of heroin wasn't enough to get me stoned and the thought of using a dirty needle that was probably infected with HIV was enough to scare me.

"Fuck that!" I said in disgust, and snorted the white line I had laid out before me.

"Billy, how are you doing? You don't look so good. I've seen you with Hassan a lot lately. He's a piece of junkie scum, a trailer-trash piece of shit. I've been watching you, man, you're on the radar. Keep away from that shit," said Sugar on our daily walk to the main hospital. I had been hitting the heroin hard over the past couple of months. "Every goddamn day, I walk through five gates and get my balls searched ten times. Hey, Billy," he said with renewed emphasis, "keep away from that blueshirt, he likes to stick his finger up your ass," said Sugar as he pointed at a slimy looking trusty who was doing the routine searches.

"You like it really, don't you, Sugar?"

"Only when it's your mother," he said, grinning.

"Your mother's still swinging around poles in Patpong," I joked.

"Blow me, bitch," said Sugar, laughing. "Billy, I'm serious, man, stay away from those kind of people. I mean it, man. It's not good for you." He walked ahead of me through the gate. He was labouring the point about Hassan but I knew he had a good reason to warn me.

A week later there was a raid on building six. Drugs, weapons and phones were captured. Hassan had been found with a syringe in his locker and was sent to Hong Soi for six months. Hong Soi was a row of punishment cells located in building five. They were roughly twelve feet square and held up to twenty prisoners – all in shackles in hot, putrid conditions. Everybody feared this kind of punishment. Gang rape was common. A Singaporean guy I met had been violently raped and beaten in one of those cells and was now a walking zombie.

Hassan, however, was a regular visitor. He was suspected of having HIV but didn't care as long as he had his fix. I had no money and my debts were high but I would still borrow to use drugs.

I was always hungry and would stand in the long queues, bowl in hand, waiting for the big Nigerian known as Baba to give me a scoop of cold slop. Twice a day government food would be delivered on trolleys known as the UN truck by the Thai inmates. The food the foreigners received was usually a bland diet of rice and cabbage soup, while the Thai food was spicy as hell. If you were lucky you would find small pieces of chicken in your bowl. The Nigerians stole most of the chicken and sold it to the Thais. They had no money and were saving every penny they could by ripping off foreigners.

The Nigerians had names on their passports like you wouldn't believe. One was called Christian Dior, another Giorgio Armani. No wonder they got caught at the airport with false passports. They needed to pay immigration off once released or spend years in limbo trapped in this country with no means to get back to their home.

The Thais would re-cook the chicken that the weirdly-named Nigerians robbed from us and sell it to their friends.

If you had no money, you starved. The combination of bad food, the drugs and my wound were taking their toll on me.

19

The Crazy Room

"WILLIAM MOORE! CAN you please go to the sleeping hall," a loud voice boomed over the speakers. Good news. It seemed my request to change cell had been considered. I had been in a big cell with forty others and had requested to move to a smaller one. "Hey, Billy, what cell are you going into?" Sugar asked.

"Cell 86," I said, thinking how lucky I was that I had only waited six months.

"Cell 86? Shit, man! With Bonzo? The crazy dude from Ghana? That cell is cursed, full of nut jobs. Why do you want to go in there?"

"Where else am I going to go? I either have to stay in a big cell with a load of Thai junkies or move to a smaller cell with eight other foreigners and one Thai, who don't use drugs or want to have sex with me. What would you suggest?"

"Hell, they really want your ugly ass? They must be desperate," said Sugar.

The Thais called cell 86 "Hong Ba", the crazy room. There were ten of us, all in that small space – three Africans, an Australian, a Canadian, a Singaporean, a Malaysian, an Indian, a Thai and me.

Suleiman looked good for fifty, he was a huge black guy who came from Ghana and nominated himself the room leader.

"In this room we do not smoke.

"We do not use drugs.

"We do not use any telephone.

"We do not do nothing, you understand? Nothing! We is good people," said Suleiman, stating the cell rules.

"Who are you? You are not the room leader," screamed Bonzo, the one Sugar had warned me about.

"Quiet, I am telling him the rules."

"Don't tell me to be quiet; I am not afraid of you. I will fight you now," screamed Bonzo, standing up, puffing out his chest and tearing off his black, rimmed glasses.

"You are a madman, sit down. I am the room leader and nobody will be fighting in here," Suleiman said, with authority. "Please don't mind him, he is craze. You can sleep here, away from the madman," Suleiman said, making space next to him. The cell was really small but it was kept clean.

"Yes, don't be minding him, he is number one not so well, he is losing his screws and missing his marbles. His tenancy here is very long, maybe twenty-years," said a young, slim Indian man, sitting opposite me. "My name is Sunail. I am pleasing to meet your company," he said, shaking his head in a way only Indians do.

I liked Sunail immediately. He had an innocence surrounding him. He had been given a fifteen-year sentence for murder. He told me the story of how he had travelled to Thailand seven years ago, to work with his uncle in a top hotel. He was a virgin. His only sexual experience was with a vibrating vagina, a twenty-first birthday present from a friend.

He met a prostitute, fell in love and was later charged with murder when a threesome he was having with his girlfriend's friend went wrong. The girlfriend became jealous; like most Thai women she was insecure. A fight broke out between the girls. The naked Sunail watched, holding his now shrivelling balls, while his girlfriend stabbed the other woman twenty-five times, killing her instantly.

Sunail, who is not the brightest spark on the planet, fled Thailand, taking his prostitute girlfriend with him to India to meet his parents. He returned six months later to help renew his girlfriend's visa and was arrested and charged along with his girlfriend for the woman's murder.

"I have been here now for seven damn years. It was for the girls and the sex. I hate the girls and the sex is all they provide, nothing more. I hate these buffaloes," Sunail said, his anger making his voice rise an octave higher.

"You are a small man with a small brain," laughed Suleiman. "You have to let Jesus come into your life. He can save you," he said, patting his black bible.

"Suleiman, what is it you are saying? I am a Hindu, my friend, you are a Christian; that is your religion," objected Sunail, frowning.

"You are a madman, you talk too much," Suleiman countered. "The only way through the gates of heaven is through Jesus." Suleiman seemed to be on a roll and was preaching from his bible loudly.

"Leave the boy alone, just read your bible to yourself, and be quiet. You are disturbing the room with your noise," said Bonzo.

"Madman, nobody is disturbing the room but you," shouted Suleiman.

"You are a madman and a coward," Bonzo, spat back.

"Hey, you guys, can you both be quiet? I am trying to read my book," said the skinny Canadian called Chris, a convicted paedophile in his early thirties with bad skin and known worldwide as the infamous Mr Swirly.

"Who are you talking to? Disgusting baby killer, I will beat you," screamed Bonzo at the top of his fifty-six year old lungs, causing the rest of the building to scream back, "Shut up, you crazies."

"I will not allow you to intimidate me, Bonzo. I will report you to the building chief if you continue to threaten me. Now can you please be quiet," said the Canadian as he continued calmly to read his book.

"You horrible kiddie raper, you will die if you say one more word."

"Shut up, you big silverback. I love kids," said the paedophile with a filthy grin.

"Silverback!" said Bonzo. "Are you calling me a gorilla? I am going to beat you."

"Quiet, please. I beg you. Nobody is going to beat no one in this room. We have to live together like decent human beings," pleaded Suleiman.

I observed what was going on and couldn't help but laugh. I understood now why this was called the crazy room. Sunail was giggling madly to himself while shaking his head.

"Everybody is crazy, my friend, don't you agree, Mister Billy? You stay here, you will be not finding your marbles too," Sunail stated.

I couldn't believe anyone in the cell didn't take drugs; the arguments went on all night, bottles were smashed, screams and curses were shouted. It was like pistols at dawn at the OK Corral.

Before dawn the prayers began. First it was the Buddhists, chanting their sutras. Then twenty minutes later the "Athan" intoned the Islamic call to prayer, the Fajar.

Allah hu Akbar Allah hu Akba
Allah hu Akbar Allah hu Akbar
Ash-hadu an-la ila ha-illallah
Ash-hadu al-la ila ha-illallah
God is great, God is great.
I bear witness that there is no God but Allah.

My eyes opened to the sound of quiet mumbling. It was Suleiman on his knees, his eyes tightly shut with his hands in prayer and facing a picture of Jesus. To the other side of me was the small Thai man, in a seated position, rocking slowly back and forth with his palms pressed together in front of him. Bonzo had his Muslim skull cap on and was on his knees, with his hands held out high in front of him, muttering indecipherable words to his God. Sunail was prostrated in front of a picture he had painstakingly drawn of a woman's genitals.

"Sunail, what are you doing?" I asked, bewildered.

"I am praying to God, the God of sex, my friend," he said very seriously.

"Why?"

"Why not, my friend, I was made by sex, I like sex and sex bring me to prison. And one day I will go back to having sex," he said with conviction.

"OK, good for you, Sunail," I said, with a puzzled look on my face and thinking that only last night he hated the sex and all the problems it caused him. Now he was praying to it. I couldn't wait for the trusty to open the cell door.

Later, Sunail asked me like it was a normal question to ask in a man's prison: "Mr Billy, do you have lady friend in the prison?"

"What! Are you serious? There's no ladies in here," I replied, although some of those fellas with tits, stilettos and thongs looked very attractive to me after I'd been banged up for a while. However, they would always be men.

"Yes, but ladyboy very sexy, do you not think so?" giggled Sunail. "Do you not miss the jiggy jiggy?" As he jumped around and rotated his hips, he received a round of applause and laughter from the rest of the room. It was good to laugh. Even Bonzo joined in.

Once the laughter had died down, Sunail sat cross-legged opposite me and looked at me seriously.

"I have very good friend who work in building nine and if you have no lady friend and feel lonely maybe I can help you, Mr Billy."

He must have seen the confusion on my face. "Help me? How?" I asked, wondering where this was leading.

"On Valentine's Day we can go to the pig farm and jiggy jiggy with the best pig there for only 1,000 baht," he said and I could see he was deadly serious.

"You're fuckin' nuts," I said, laughing out loud.

"No, jing jing. My friend he is blueshirt and work there. I yet to try. I am very shy, you see, and would like it if you came along with me."

Suleiman broke into fits of laughter: "You are a madman. You have to go into that toilet with a tissue and sort yourself out. Nobody is fucking pigs around here, you filthy man," he said between sniggers.

I have never laughed so much in my life and it was the laughter and the madness that surrounded me that kept me alive and fed my spirit. It was either laugh or cry.

"Was that your cell bitching last night? Goddamn, I don't know how you sleep, man," Sugar asked me on our walk to the hospital.

"Yeah, they're all nuts, arguing over nothing. It has to be better than my last cell though," I said.

"Nobody in that cell wants your ugly ass, then?" Sugar chuckled.

"Shut it, fat tits," I said, smiling. "Sugar, what's the Thai word for infection? My feet are green," I said, showing him the soles of my feet.

"Ohoo, that looks painful, man. 'Mee kway tiem krap', that means infection," Sugar said "The nurse will understand."

I should have known not to trust Sugar! I had asked the nurse if she had a vibrator. She was not amused. It was about time I learnt more Thai and improved my communication skills.

20

Struggling to Survive

"BILLY, CAN YOU borrow any money? I have good heroin," said Fat Tony, a young Italian with the bluest eyes I have ever seen. He showed me a straw, ten centimetres in length, that was full of white powder. "We can share, this is very good shit, man," Tony said, while shaking the straw.

"I owe everyone money. I don't think anyone is going to front me any more until I've cleared my debts. Can you wait until Kathleen visits? You know she'll be here in the next couple of weeks," I said, hoping against hope that he would say yes, and hating the sound of my own pleading voice. Kathleen the missionary came to Bangkok every two months to visit the people she knew from Chiang Mai. Fat Tony was on her list as he had spent some time there.

"No problem, my friend, I wait. But two cartons of cigarettes, OK? We do 2,000 baht between us," said Tony.

I followed Tony to the far corner of the building, close to the library, where the Samurai gangs hung out.

"Tony, what are we doing here? Why don't we go to the locker room?" I said, looking around nervously.

"The locker room is too dangerous. It has many cameras, my friend," replied Tony.

Too dangerous! This was really dangerous, pulling out a straw filled with heroin on the Samurai gang's patch.

"Are you mad, Tony?"

"It's OK, I buy from them," he said, while setting up a line on the cover of an old magazine. A few haggard members of the gang were heading towards us, rapidly approaching.

"Quick, Tony they're coming," I said, grabbing a straw and pushing him out of the way. I greedily snorted up the huge white line. It was gone before they arrived. Tony was already burning one end of the straw in a mad panic.

"Shit, shit, shit," mouthed Tony, "this is not good."

Not good! We were surrounded by a mob of disease-infected Samurais holding dirty blood-filled syringes. They spoke to Tony, who couldn't understand a word of what was being said. Terror was written all over his face and he was visibly shaking. By this time my Thai was pretty good so I translated to Tony what they were saying.

"Tony, they want the heroin and they want it now," I said. "Tony, listen to me, mate, they're saying they'll inject us both with HIV if you don't hand over that straw."

Tony didn't reply. He just charged forward like a madman, dodging the growing crowd. He was screaming like a banshee. The mob stormed after him, leaving me alone. Fat Tony was like a rampaging elephant and knocked them down like skittles.

I knew at that point I had to stop using drugs. I was either going to die a horrible death at the hands of these gangs or go insane.

Roman the Russian was very strange indeed; he had a young, fresh face that was carefully hidden from the sun with a scruffy blue cap. He gazed upon me with shifty, blue eyes the very first day I walked into building six. We never spoke, but Sugar warned me about him.

"Shit, man, Roman the Russian, ex-KGB, the piece of shit: be careful, he's a thief. I'm sure he stole my socks off the line," snarled Sugar, as Roman's shifty eyes were cast upon us with deep suspicion.

"Don't trust that idiot. Did you know that he shags ladyboys then steals from them? Yeah, man, that's his charge, shagging guys and stealing their stuff, but what happened this one time was that Roman didn't count on getting beat up by one of these guys with titties. He was beaten and dragged downtown to the police station and charged with robbery and assault on ladyboys. He was given fifteen years. The faggot should have gotten life," spat Sugar in disgust.

I never knew whether to believe Sugar's bullshit and decided to form my own opinion about people.

It wasn't long before I encountered Roman the Russian for myself. It was about a month after arriving in building six. He approached me slowly, his eyes darting back and forth, as if he was suspicious of being watched.

He stood next to me for a short while saying absolutely nothing, and then suddenly I realized he was attempting to speak to me. I could barely hear his voice, as he was whispering out of the side of his mouth, almost secretly.

"I have been watching you and I have made the decision to allow you to come into my cell," whispered Roman.

"Is that right?" I heard myself whisper and then suddenly thought how bizarrely I was behaving, responding in this manner.

"Yes it is true, I see you look like a clean person and I would be happy if you came into my cell. You cannot stay with those other prisoners, they are crazy," Roman continued to whisper as if being heard was a problem.

"I'll think about it," I whispered back. Roman stared at me, making me feel uneasy. He was certainly a strange one. I watched as he walked away, his eyes continually looking everywhere at the same time. I instantly formed the opinion that he was nuts.

Sugar frowned when I told him what Roman had suggested. "Hey, I don't think you will last long with him as a cellmate, no one likes him, crazy nut job," he snorted.

The next day Roman walked over to me and asked me about my decision. "Would you like to move into my cell? I can arrange a move for you today," said Roman.

"Roman, thanks for the offer, but I want to share a cell with my friend Scott," I told him, hoping he would understand and that his feelings weren't hurt, like I really cared. Roman said nothing; he just shook his head up and down as if in deep thought, then walked away still silent.

Sugar wobbled over, his huge stomach out in front of him. "Hey, Billy, did you tell that crack job where to go? He didn't look too pleased," laughed Sugar.

"I told him I was moving in with Scott, or at least I wanted to. He's definitely a disturbed character. Some mothers do have them, and this is the place you meet them, I guess."

"Yeah, too true, bro, this place creates insanity. I mean, take a look over there," said Sugar, pointing at a group of cripples and sick people. "What kind of cruel people treat cripples in wheelchairs, with no goddamn legs, the same as everybody else? We even have a blind person in here, God knows why he's here, but shit, man, I mean this isn't normal," said Sugar, shaking his head sadly.

It was true, I could never imagine people being treated in the UK the same way as these sick and crippled inmates. They would be placed in a hospital or a mental institution, not made to hobble around in rags or sit in busted wheelchairs. These people's treatment was scandalous.

I remembered a guy named Gog who was in Chiang Mai prison and had to wear a head guard to protect himself from all the knocks and bangs he would take due to the heavy doses of medication he was on. Gog was beaten to near death eight years ago when he first got remanded in prison for the murder of his parents. If Thais despise anything it's people who murder their parents because family is very important to them. Gog survived the beating, but suffered terrible brain damage and you would often see him pulling down his shorts and shitting on the hot concrete floor. He would wobble and slobber all the time and was always covered with cuts and bruises.

Gog's treatment was inhumane; however, there was nothing that could be done about it. Nan told me that Gog had never been to court in the eight years he had been there. He was too mentally unstable to stand trial, so he was left to rot with no hope of ever being freed. That was in Chiang Mai prison. My new home, Klong Prem, was worse and was full of mentally-unstable, crazed killers. I felt as if I was walking on broken glass, with the fear of upsetting the wrong person.

A Thai friend named Nee, whom I had met while sitting in the library, wanted me to teach him English and in return he would help me read and write the Thai language. He was an ex-prison guard who had been convicted of supplying ya ba and given four years. He was in his early fifties and could speak pretty good English, but wanted to improve his vocabulary.

He lent me a Thai-English dictionary; it was an expensive book that taught spoken Thai the polite way. I felt privileged to be given the opportunity to use this book, and would hide it in the library each evening before we were locked in our cells. I would then retrieve it the next day. However, on this one day when I went to the library to get Nee's book, it was gone! Panic enveloped me, suffocating the life out of my body. Where had it gone? I searched every inch of the library and asked Pi Chet if he had moved it. Of course he hadn't, he told me.

Nee bounced into the library ten minutes later with the usual smile spread across his happy face and his exercise book under his arm.

"Good morning, teacher Billy, are you ready to study?" asked Nee.

"Nee, your dictionary has been stolen," I said, and looked at the floor, not wanting to make eye contact.

"Arai wa? How? By whom? Don't worry, teacher Billy, we will find it. I will announce it over the Tannoy. Maybe someone picked it up by mistake," said Nee hopefully.

Only fifteen minutes later, Nee was heard asking in Thai for whoever had his dictionary to return it as it was not a library book. One of Nee's friends told us he had heard that Roman was trying to sell a Thai-English dictionary. On hearing this news, I made my way over to the canteen where Roman was usually playing chess with one of his Malaysian cellmates.

"Can I have a word with you, Roman?" I said.

"Yes of course. How may I assist you?" Roman offered.

"You can assist me by returning the book you stole from the library. Don't deny it. I was told that you tried to sell Nee's dictionary and I want it back, thank you," I said calmly, even though I was raging deep inside.

"What did you say? I am not a thief and I do not have your book," Roman said defiantly.

Just at that moment Nee arrived with his friend who pointed the finger at Roman. "You have his book. I know, because you tried to sell it to me," Nee's friend accused the now angry red-faced Roman.

"I do not know what you are saying. I have no book," Roman continued to deny any knowledge of it.

"Now listen, you thief, if you don't give it back by lunchtime, you're going to have a problem, understand?" I said to Roman, the anger bubbling up inside of me.

"Ha! Do you think I am afraid of you? Shall we step outside and discuss this?"

I followed Roman outside, my fists clenched ready for action, when all of a sudden he ran as fast as he could to the building chief's office, just like the coward he was.

My name was called over the Tannoy minutes after Roman entered the office. I asked Nee to accompany me and translate to the building chief what had happened. Roman denied the theft, the book was never returned and Roman continued to steal anything and everything to support his ever growing ice habit. It dampened the heart to know that even in prison your belongings were not safe from your fellow inmates.

Just before I was repatriated back to the UK, I happened to see Roman take a terrible beating from a group of Thai inmates – for stealing from them, I was told. In my book, that was no more than he deserved. Roman had got away with too much for too long and had finally gone too far.

Back in cell 86, the arguing continued every night without respite, and I watched amused at the way Suleiman and Bonzo threatened each other. It was usually over the TV which was useless to a load of foreigners who couldn't understand a word of it anyway. To me, the TV was just background noise.

"Bonzo, please I beg you, we want to watch the news," pleaded Suleiman.

"Why don't you be quiet and stop disturbing me? I am watching my programme," said Bonzo, ignoring Suleiman's pleas.

"Yes, I agree with Mr Suleiman, we would like to watch the news," giggled Sunail.

"Who are you? Are we friends? Do I know you? I'm not your friend," shouted Bonzo, "so please stop all your noise. You're disturbing me!"

"Hey, guys, can you all be quiet? Just switch the TV off," said Jason, the paedophile from Australia.

"Shut up, baby killer. I will smash this TV over your head," screamed Bonzo, who suddenly pulled the small portable from the wall and raised it above his head. This prompted the paedophile to jump up from his place on the floor and puff out his chest. The vile creature wasn't small and he had a rich daddy who took care of him, buying him what he needed to survive in a Thai prison. He had his protein and supplements and trained alone in the makeshift gym that the foreigners built.

"You are a coward, Bonzo. I dare you to hit me with that TV," the paedophile said quietly.

Suleiman quickly got to his feet to help calm the situation, holding his hands up high in surrender. "Please, I beg you, let us behave like decent human beings. Put down the TV. Are you crazy?" said Suleiman, staring hard into Bozo's eyes.

"Yes, I am crazy and I am not afraid of you or anyone else," said Bonzo, finally putting down the TV.

This type of thing happened almost all the time – screams, shouts, empty threats, but never any actual violence. It killed a lot of time and was better than any movie I had ever seen. But I was out of that cell like a shot every morning and kept well away from everyone else.

Not long after our encounter with these drug-crazed junkies, I witnessed and watched as another man no older than twenty-five was stabbed to death. I could see he had no chance of escape as the knife was sinking deep into his body. The blade was at least nine inches long, the attack didn't seem frenzied, more cold and calculated and the inhuman sounds coming from the victim were frightening. He was like a trapped animal with no place to run.

I was yards away and, as I watched, time seemed to slow down. Another man ran past me with a chair and hit the stabbed man over the head. This was cold-blooded murder. The crowd watching this vicious killing numbered at least fifty. I heard shouts of "kaa man" and "teng kao", which I knew translated as "kill it" and "stab him." It was as if to say that this boy, a human being, was no more than a diseased dog that needed to be put down. The atmosphere felt evil.

No one attempted to intervene or rescue the poor boy from this murderous onslaught. I couldn't take my eyes off the knife as it entered his body over and over again, the blood squirting everywhere. I was fascinated, which caused a brief moment of guilt at the sight of this boy being killed.

I hadn't used drugs for a couple of months now and all my debts were cleared. I am a man of extremes. If I use, I use everything and if I stop, I stop everything.

No half measures.

I had made the decision to live. I wanted to get out of that hell-hole alive and see my family one more time. It had been years since I had seen them, although my mother kept in touch via mail as did my good friend René. I so badly wanted to see them and be amongst family and friends again. The one friend I missed the most was Jason. He was the older brother I never had but always wanted. We were close before I left England but had lost contact once I chose to pick up drugs. He didn't even know where I was. I would often wonder, will I ever see him again? I held onto the hope that I would and fought with my feelings on a daily basis to stay clean.

"What's wrong with him, Sugar?" I said, pointing at a young Thai boy who was stalking me.

"Shit, man, he's OK. I guess he wants to be your buddy," replied Sugar. "Hey, Job, tam arai? Kuhn sabai dee ru bplao?" (What are you doing? Are you OK?) he asked the boy, who just shrugged his shoulders and plodded off, saying nothing, his battered old sandals slapping hard against the concrete.

"He's a nutter, him, mate. He's in for killing a policeman. I asked him why, and do you know what he said? He said he shot him because he was bothering him," said Ste, a Brit who came from the north of England and was serving twenty years for a drug offence. "He's not the full ticket, him, lad. He follows everyone everywhere. You can't even have a shit in peace because he pops up to bum food off you. Just don't bother him and you'll be alright," he said, coughing and spluttering on one of his homemade cigarettes.

"You want to sort those lungs out," I laughed, as he spat a thick, green blob of phlegm into the filthy drain.

"I know, but I love these lung busters," he said, pushing himself out of his improvised deck chair, the effort causing him to grimace in pain.

"What's wrong, lad?" I asked him.

"It's me leg, I've got all this green pus coming out of it," he said, pulling down the dirty bandage that was covering the wound on his shin. "Look at that! It was only a spot last week, now it's just getting bigger."

It looked a mess. I had seen infections similar to this one in the prison hospital. I knew that if he didn't get proper treatment, he could lose his leg.

"Still off the swag, Bill?" Ste, asked me, referring to the heroin.

"Yeah, still off it, mate, the cigarettes too," I said. I was feeling better about not being beaten by the drugs and having to live with the shame of begging for food and smokes.

"Ya need to sort that leg out, lad. It looks manky."

Ste just looked at me. Sadness and defeat followed him around like the grim reaper. The sentence he was serving stole any hope he had of surviving with his health or sanity intact.

Everybody was taking some sort of drug in one form or another. The damage was already done to most. I was a survivor, a born fighter. No one had to visit hell alive, I thought. And that's what this place was, a living hell.

One thing I had learnt about being banged up in a Thai prison was that there was nothing that could scare me anymore.

Pichet was a small man in his early fifties, with big, powerful shoulders and a warm, open smile that said, "You can ask me anything you want, I've heard it all before." He was in charge of maintaining the library and helped the foreigners with complaints, not that they were ever replied to and more often than not ended up in the bin.

"Sawatdee krap, Kuhn Billy, how are you today?" he asked me when I entered the library. He was sitting at a table laden with mouth-watering delights. There was somtam, a spicy papaya salad popular amongst the Thais, beef, sweet-and-sour chicken and a wide variety of vegetables, all served with soft boiled rice.

"Sit, please join us, eat," he said, gesturing to the exotic delights laid before my eyes. My stomach was rumbling. It had been quite some time since I had eaten food of this quality. It looked great.

"Don't mind if I do," I said, sitting down quickly before he changed his mind. "I'm starving, I could eat a scabby dog, not that this looks like dog food."

Pichet just smiled and asked Abu and Hafiz, his Malaysian helpers, to set up a plate of food and fetch me a bottle of ice-cold water. They responded immediately and were very polite. I felt like I was in the best restaurant in Bangkok. I could get used to this, I thought. If I stayed away from the drugs it could very much be this way.

"You want to pray with us before we begin?" Pichet asked me. He and the Malaysian helpers were devout Muslims. I thought about all the wonderful food on the table and then the praying thing. I hated all that Allah and God stuff but what harm could a little prayer do?

"Yeah, of course, no problem," I said and joined my hands together in the only way I knew prayers were said.

"No, like this," Abu said, holding his hands out in front of him, palms facing upwards.

"Hafiz, you say the prayer," said Pichet. Hafiz started praying and I watched as everyone placed their hands out in front of them. I did the same, feeling really uncomfortable.

"Bishmilla hi rok man nir ror heem..." Hafiz prayed in a language I had never heard before.

The food was the best thing I had tasted since the Embassy had treated us the Christmas before to cold hamburgers and fries from MacDonald's. I joined Pichet and the Malaysians for lunch each day after the midday prayers. I would join them in the mosque and copy what they did when they prayed.

In the beginning, I did it for the wonderful food we would eat after the prayer. However, I soon began to feel a change in my behaviour. I went to the Juma prayers on a Friday in the education block; this is where I met Mitch, an Australian who had converted to Islam seven years before. We were the only two Western Muslims in the prison and we got a lot of funny looks.

Mitch is a very interesting fellow who had received the death sentence for drug offences which had been commuted to forty years. The Americans also wanted him for suspected internet drug deals. The thing is, the internet was just becoming news in 1993 when Mitch came to prison. He told me he had never used a computer before prison, so I asked him how he could have done what the yanks accused him of. He said that the guards from Bangkwang stood up in court and testified that it was impossible for this prisoner to have a laptop and mobile phone, but the court granted the extradition anyway.

After he finished his sentence in Thailand, Mitch would have to go to America and begin the whole shit process again over there. You would have thought that this would depress him; in fact he was confident that no court in the world with any sense would convict him of this alleged crime.

Mitch was the only foreigner I had met who never allowed this hell we lived in to get him down. He was very much a man who had it together. He was over six feet tall, with broad shoulders. He was very intelligent and liked by almost everyone in the prison, except the guards as he would often voice his opinions in an appropriate manner. He had been in prison for seventeen years and was now forty-four years old. We became good friends and still remain so even today.

"I heard you're a rag head," Ste said one day after I had finished lunch with Pichet, Abu and Hafiz.

"What? You're mad, aren't you?" I replied. "They're good people anyway and I enjoy their company, that's all. They're not what I thought Muslims would be like. Do you know what, I'd say they were the kindest people you could meet in here." I said this with conviction and I meant it. I had only seen Muslims portrayed as terrorists, hijacking planes or carrying backpacks full of bombs. But no, not the Muslims I had met. They greeted each other with the traditional salaam and helped anyone, regardless of their religion, status or lack of it.

"So are you a Muslim now?" Ste asked me casually. "Do a bit of carpet flapping, you and the midget Muslim Pichet?" He was obviously on a wind-up today.

"You've got to pray five times a day. It's a very strict religion, Billy, or should I call you Mohammed Ali now? He joked, but with seriousness in his voice. "And you can't smoke or shag ladyboys; you can't do anything," he continued. "Do you know what, mate? I once gave up sex and drugs and it was the scariest twenty minutes of my life." He was so funny sometimes. I walked away and left him chuckling to himself as he delved into the depths of his drug-dazed memory bank.

Most mornings I stayed in the library where Pichet worked. His job was to maintain the books in the foreign section and it was the only place that had fans and a decent place to sit. I would sit and read the noble Koran and learn to pray in Arabic with the help of Hafiz. I eventually moved into Pichet's room and prayed five times a day. It helped me and made me want to be a better person. Most people thought I was blagging it, but I knew I needed fear in my heart to keep me sane and on the right path.

The situation I was in at the time was one of chaos and confusion; I was just keeping the engine room running. I needed to get my health back because I was so damaged physically, mentally and spiritually. This spurred me to fight for my survival. I was ill and weak and needed good food to regain my strength before I could even start doing anything.

Religion! I would have believed in anything – ghouls, goblins, even fairy tales – just to feel safe and protected and have a decent meal inside me. I was sick and tired of the mud soup and sticky rice.

I realised now that it was the safest place for me to be. I wrapped myself in the Islamic religion out of fear. Yes, it was self-seeking, but there was so much conflict going on inside me, the murders and rapes were traumatising to say the least and the prison was a hovel of hatred and disease.

I knew I was confused the day I turned up with a skirt on, a skull cap and a carpet over my shoulder. And I had a new name, Yousuf Mohamed Ali. It sounds crazy now, but in the five years I had been in Thailand, I had changed my religion half a dozen times. I'd been Catholic, simply Christian, Buddhist, atheist and Muslim. I was just trying to find a way out.

My addiction was out of control and the desperation, loneliness and isolation I was feeling crucified me on a daily basis.

I was so raw at times I felt like a bare bulb without a shade.

They say you can fool a baker and get away with a bun, but if you fool yourself you'll end with none. The reality was that I knew there was a way out. Jails, psychiatry, religion and medicine were not that answer, it was the fellowship of Narcotics Anonymous that had saved my life and those of countless others. I just needed to get back home.

A story I heard once kept repeating itself in my head. The story goes like this: A hopeless drug addict was trapped down a hole with no way out. He screamed and shouted for help, when along came a doctor. The addict begged the doctor to help him, so he did what he knew best and wrote out a prescription, smiled, then walked away.

The hopeless addict again began screaming for help, tears streaming down his face, when along came a counsellor. He sat down above the hole and talked to the addict for one hour, then wished him all the best and moved on.

"Help!" roared the addict, "I need to get out!" Another addict, who had been clean for a number of years, stopped by and looked down at this hopeless creature, pleading for help. The clean addict jumped down into the hole. The desperate addict looked at him as if he was crazy and said, "Now we're both lost." With that, he fell to his knees and sobbed uncontrollably.

The clean addict picked him up and gave him a huge hug. "It's OK," he said. "Follow me. I know a way out."

Like the clean addict, I knew the answer and had the tools I needed. The trouble was, I had misplaced them. Until I could get them back, I knew that I had to survive any way I could whilst in prison.

"Mr Billy, I need you to help I. Me am not understanding this word 'gratitude'. I speak correctly, yes?" asked Mr Lee. He was Korean and he was pointing to a word he had found in his Bible. We were sitting in the library. I had my usual morning coffee in my hand and was answering his English questions, not really in the mood. He was a strange one, that Mr Lee, and very dangerous. We didn't seem to get on too well. There was a little history between us. We either hated each other or loved each other. Mostly it was hate.

You wouldn't believe where I met Mr Lee. It was under a blanket, smoking ice. Now Mr Lee is not someone you would want to upset. They called him Mr Sushi and not because he was good with fish. This madman chopped his friend up into eight pieces over an argument. He was high on methamphetamine at the time and, in one drug-fuelled night of madness, he slaughtered his friend at a hotel in Pattaya. He was caught trying to smuggle the body out in suitcases and was sentenced to twenty-five years. And my introduction into his world was under a blanket, smoking the same drug that caused him to commit this gruesome crime.

"I no smoke ice no more, not good for head me, two months now I no take. Now I happy, I have my Bible. Do you know this guy Jesus? You know about his life?" he said, looking hard into my eyes. Mr Lee was nuts, and he disliked the fact that I was now a Muslim. We were close to fighting on more than one occasion. If the truth was known, he was scary and I didn't fancy fighting with him, so would just walk away when it became too heated.

I counted each minute of every day. Time dragged on and the sun beat down hard. Sweat poured down my face in streams, the salt blinding me as it fell into my eyes.

Bangkok is the hottest city on the face of this planet, due to the smog and pollution covering the city in a thick blanket of smoke. All I could do was suffer the heat and plod on.

Job followed me everywhere; I felt sorry for him, he reminded me of my younger brother Joey, who was mentally handicapped.

Job should never have been placed in a prison. He was not well and had the mental age of someone much younger than his 22 years; he was like a child and I felt very protective of him. How he was still alive confused me. He had been shot five times by the police and spent nine months in the hospital. On the day he was discharged he was knocked down by a bus and spent a further seven months in the hospital.

Job had been sentenced to forty years for the murder of a police officer whom he had shot because he annoyed him; the police officer he shot dead was nothing but a bully.

Job had the oldest pair of flip-flops I had ever seen, which were split in the front and flopped with a crack on the hot concrete floor.

"You need new shoes," I said, pointing at his flip-flops. He stood still, with a look of confusion on his poor, sad, child-like face. Snot dribbled from his nose, he was half-naked and his thin body was covered in prison tats.

"Huh," he grunted.

"Rong tow, seer lao," (your shoes are no good) I said slowly, hoping he would understand my Thai.

"Roo lao," (I know) he grunted loudly.

"Suer mai, na," (buy new ones) I told him.

He just looked at me, then looked down at his feet, took off both of his flip-flops, lovingly stared at them, gave them a kiss and, with all his strength, threw them over the wall into the hospital grounds. A huge smile adorned his face. "OK," he shouted, overjoyed at his decision to throw away his old flip-flops. He gave me the thumbs-up and marched quickly away, waving his arms in the air and singing a Thai song loudly and out of tune.

It is early, 7.15am, and something's going on! The atmosphere has changed; small groups of prisoners are all heading in one direction. Where are they going? What's going on now?

Follow the blood trail, that's usually a tell-tale sign of a problem. A small tattooed guy walks past me, blood leaking out of multiple wounds. Two trusties escort him to the building chief's office; six others go off in search of the other offender. He's been apprehended. No wounds are visible. I've seen him before, injecting heroin in the locker room. HIV is written all over his ravaged, tattooed body. I see him sitting outside the office. A small crowd gathers round to watch.

"Where's the weapon?" the guard shouts. The prisoner says nothing; a huge, black boot slams into his lower back, forcing the wind out of him. Still he remains quiet. "The weapon!" the guard screams again.

No need to ask any more questions. The trusties have found it, a long, nasty knife. The Thai takes another kick from the guard and screams out in pain. He is then dragged into the office. The trusty now has a camera; he and the knife follow the prisoner inside and the door is closed. It's over.

Or is it?

The office door flies open again. Trusties and guards come running out, fear etched on their faces, quickly followed by the prisoner, the knife he used in the attack held to his own throat. There are visible puncture wounds around his chest and abdomen, vigorously pumping out thick red blood. He's close by; the crowd scatter in fear.

He has a resigned look in his eyes. He's going to die anyway. Nobody attempts to go near him, the blood alone is enough to frighten anyone. I walk away; I need a coffee.

Before, "crazy" used to mean something but these days everybody's crazy. This is how it was; it didn't affect me anymore. I just watched as everybody else went completely mad. How I stayed sane is a mystery to me, maybe I was just a madman thinking I was sane. They say a psychotic is someone who has just found out what's going on. That's probably what I did, the day I stopped the drugs.

Rob, a British guy, had been sentenced to twenty years imprisonment for the murder of a Scottish man on the island of Koh Samui. He always denied the crime and claimed that the murder was actually committed by the man's own Thai girlfriend. Rob had been in prison for seven years when I first met him in building six. He was a tall, good-looking kid, tanned from years in the baking sun. He had lost two appeals and had one more chance; his last hope lay with the highest court in the country. He was confident that the Thai judicial system would see sense and give him back his freedom. But remember this was Thailand and the Thais don't need much evidence, if any, to convict you. Personally, I thought the odds were stacked against him, and any chances of winning his final appeal were low.

In fact Rob lost his appeal and had thirteen years left before release – thirteen years of hot, sweaty boredom in the fires of hell! I watched as he relied on drugs. He became friends with Fat Tony. Tony was self-centred, self-seeking and manipulative. His only goal in life was to get stoned, on other people's money. He reminded me a lot of myself. I'd been there so I could tolerate his bollix, but only just.

This unlikely friendship between Rob and Tony was doomed from the beginning. Rob would use crystal meth (ice) sociably at the weekends, but Tony was a drug monster and was forever in debt due to his massive drug habit. His family sent him money every couple of months so he could clear his debts and he was trusted by the dealers and money lenders of Lard Yao to pay on time.

Soon the weekend drug use extended to weekdays. Rob was always very talkative and seemed happy. The ice allowed him to escape the concrete hell he was in.

One day, after a couple of months of daily abusing his body and mind with this drug, he went mad. He sat in his chair and had long conversations with himself. I approached him one day, worried about his mental state.

"Hello, Rob. How are you, mate?"

"Don't you know it's rude to interrupt when someone is talking? Have you not got any manners?"

I looked into his eyes. They were wild, Rob was gone, and in his place was a madman.

"I'm sorry, mate, you're right. Forgive me for being rude."

"Now, look here, old boy, work has to be done so be gone with you," he said.

Rob became a problem with the other foreigners who shared his cell. They feared for their safety because he was a convicted murderer who had threatened to kill everybody in the cell as they slept.

"What are we going to do with him, Bill?" asked Ste. "He's nuts. We can't sleep in the same cell."

We could only watch as he slipped more deeply into his madness; he drank the filthy sewer water that ran past the toilets, chewed on dustbin lids, he even ate the building chief's flowers. We had to get him help before he was badly injured or even killed.

The decision was made to confront the building chief as we needed to get Rob into a hospital, preferably with padded cells. We took him to the office and pleaded with the building chief to send him to hospital. The chief was a decent man who was willing to help the foreigners. Unfortunately, Rob, being crazy, lit up a cigarette and blew a thick plume of smoke into the building chief's face, who became enraged.

"You no smoke!" he screamed, spittle coming out of his mouth. "You no good man, you no respect," he spat in broken English.

"Rob, chill out, man. Get rid of that ciggie, mate," Ste told him.

"We don't want no trouble, sir. He's sick and needs help," we said.

Rob put the cigarette out on his tongue and began eating it, as the building chief looked on in disbelief. Next, Rob stood to attention, saluted, sang the British national anthem at the top of his lungs, did an about-turn and marched out of the office.

"Crazy farang," the building chief muttered as he signed the papers to send poor Rob to the fourth floor of the prison hospital where all the mental patients were.

Rob was an interesting character, and the events that led up to his incarceration and subsequent decline make compelling reading.

Rob woke up at about 7.00am; this was going to be the day that changed his life. He stood and looked out through his open window, smelled the sweet sea air and admired the beautiful palm trees. It was a day like any other day. He made a cup of coffee and went out onto his balcony, sat in his bamboo chair and soaked up the wonderful view. After his morning coffee, he played a few songs on his acoustic guitar, feeling free and alive. His house was only one of two built on the mountain behind the point where Maenam and Bophut beaches meet to form a point between two bays. From his balcony he could see both beaches in their entirety, and further out there was a statue of a big Buddha, over which the sun rose into the sky each morning. Across the sea was the island of Koh Phangan. During the day, Phangan was various shades of green, and at night it gave a dazzling show of rainbow lights. On either side, reaching far out into the sea, there were hundreds of lights from the fishing boats earning their catch.

Rob's house was just over a quarter of the way up the mountain, just before it got too steep to build. His next-door neighbour, a Chinese man named Joe, lived about 500 meters further down the mountain. The mountain belonged to a Thai family who allowed Rob to live in the house with only one neighbour, so it was very peaceful and serene. The dirt track stopped at the house, so no one ever came up the hill apart from a few close friends he would invite at different times.

Rob had a French friend who came around a lot, usually on one of his quad bikes. The French guy and his brother owned the quad track at the back of the mountain and rented out the bikes. They also owned a bar and had Sky TV with music channels playing most of the time. Rob spent a lot of his time at the bar, eating and drinking for free.

He had been living in the house for about eight months and the area surrounding it was overgrown and the dirt track leading up to it was dangerous with rocks and boulders protruding from the ground, so he had to be careful when riding his moped. Most of his time was spent clearing up the dirt track with the help of his neighbour Joe. Once he had the route cleared, he would take his guitar up to the top of the mountain where he also had a hammock fitted, so sometimes he would spend the night there and wait for the sun to rise behind the big Buddha, chilling out and playing his guitar.

One night while Rob was playing pool in the bar, three Thai girls came in. They wanted to play as well, so that was how they spent the rest of the evening, besides drinking and singing. Two of the girls were sisters and the other a friend. During the evening, the sisters' friend left, and Rob decided to go home to bed as he was beat. To his surprise, the two sisters asked if they could come home with him. They followed him on their motorbike, and upon arriving at his place, had a laugh and a few more drinks until Rob fell asleep.

When he woke up, he saw one of the sisters, named Bee, cutting open a coconut with one of his machetes on the balcony. Her sister Ploy wasn't there but, not long after, she returned with breakfast for them all. Rob was delighted and following that day, he became close with Bee. The sisters would come around to Rob's place on a regular basis, taking him around the island to sightsee and eat at open-air restaurants, so he was pretty much enjoying life with the two sisters.

Sometimes Rob would go back to Bee's bungalow where she lived with Ploy; it was just before where the slope of the mountain started. Theirs was the last bungalow down a long dirt track with high walls which stretched in a U-shape with about five bungalows along the stretch. Rob had only been there a few times and wouldn't stay long. After going to the 7-Eleven he decided to visit Bee's place to see what she was up to; she wanted to go to the waterfall with Ploy and her boyfriend. They invited Rob to go along.

Ploy and her boyfriend were off somewhere, so Rob told Bee he would call back later, and off he went. When he returned, Bee was outside her neighbour's bungalow. Rob stopped and had a laugh with her. Not long after, he saw Ploy walking up the road with someone he assumed was her boyfriend. As they passed, Rob heard them arguing. He thought it was just a domestic squabble until he heard a loud slap and looked over at Ploy. She had been struck across the face by the man.

Ploy disappeared and came back with a knife. The next thing Rob saw was the guy gripping his own throat with both hands while making gurgling sounds. Blood was spraying out between his fingers.

Rob was only yards away but, by the time he jumped off his bike and ran the few steps to him, the guy was already on the floor. He must have died within seconds. His throat was cut nearly all the way through.

Ploy was gone and Bee was screaming. Rob knew the police would arrive shortly so, as he was wanted for jumping bail on a drugs charge, he fled the scene in a mad panic. He couldn't start his bike so he ran with it until he felt composed enough to get it started, then headed for the 7-Eleven to buy some cigarettes and food. His plan was to be seen on camera with a receipt and provide himself with an alibi for the time of the killing.

Then he headed to Joe's to see what he would suggest. However, Joe was out. As Rob turned to leave, he heard a bike coming up the mountain. The police! Rob saw that the officer was armed and, to his surprise, recognised him as a friend of the sisters. Rob had seen him out with them once before, but hadn't known he was a policeman. Bee was with him and she was pointing at Rob.

The cop quickly got off his bike, pulled out his gun and aimed it at Rob's chest. He was arrested and marched down the hill to a waiting van and greeted by about a dozen policemen, lights flashing. Rob was taken back to the scene of the crime by the police. The body was just being zipped up and ready to be taken away.

Rob was treated like a savage and accused of murder. He was painfully handcuffed, hands behind his back. On the way to the police station, thinking he would be released in no time once they realized they had the wrong person, he allowed himself a brief smile. In the police station they stripped him naked while holding a gun on him. They took all his clothes and gave him a Roma football kit to wear; this he wore for three weeks.

They handed him a pen and paper, demanding he sign it; they threatened him with a meat cleaver, slamming it hard into the table so he signed their document but wrote in English under his signature that he didn't understand what he was signing. He couldn't tell the police the truth; he didn't want Ploy to get in trouble and he was confident he would be freed soon.

Rob never got bail and pleaded not guilty but was convicted of the murder of the Scottish guy and was sentenced to twenty years.

21

The Nightmare Is Over

PEOPLE FROM THE embassy came to visit the British inmates of Klong Prem every couple of months. I had put in a request to be repatriated and it looked like this had been granted. The embassy wouldn't tell me the date I was to be transferred although they knew! I was definitely going to be the last to find out.

"William, it's security. You have to understand," said Kate, who was from Australia but represented the British embassy. Kate was very attractive for her years. She was always helpful to the British inmates. She went on: "If the Thais get wind that you know your transfer date it could compromise everything, then it could all go horribly wrong. It has been known for the Thais to cancel transfers due to inmates knowing when they are going."

"OK, but at least give me some idea. It's driving me nuts, all this waiting. Is it going to be the beginning of the month, the middle, the end?" I asked, my eyes pleading, almost begging.

The days dragged on and each one seemed longer than the last; the unbearable heat got worse each day.

Kate looked around the little air-conditioned office that the Thais used for embassy meetings and moved a little closer to me. "William, I can tell you this, you will be gone by the end of the month," she said, almost whispering. She smiled when she saw my face light up.

"The end of the month?" I said to myself. As I slumped back into my chair, my heart was beating fast in my chest. I couldn't believe that, by the end of this month, after five long years away, I would be heading home, or almost home. I would have to spend a couple of months in HMP Wandsworth, an old Victorian prison in the south of London, but it was 6,000 miles closer to home than Klong Prem.

Scott was also on the visit and begged the people from the embassy to help him move back from building three to building six. He had lost a lot of weight but looked much better than he used to.

"I should be back next week, Bill," he told me. "They're off their heads over there, talking to walls, killing each other over bloody paracetamol. There is absolutely nothing available there, no drugs at all. I've been straight for six months. I've been saving my money up for when I get back to building six, when I can get proper wasted."

I guessed that this was his only reason for getting back there.

"Did you hear about Eliyas?" Scott continued. "He's off his cake. He only went and climbed a tree and tied a sarong around his neck, over Lena. He wanted to move back to building six to be with him. Trying to kill himself over a man with tits! And he's a Muslim. Isn't that supposed to be haram? I heard from Mitch that you're a Muslim now," he said, laughing.

Eliyas had tried to stab Lena in a jealous rage. So Lena smashed a glass bottle over his head. They had had many arguments in the time I had known them. But this was the worst. And they had both been punished and transferred to other parts of the prison. Eliyas had ended up in building three with Scott and was certified nuts.

One morning, I heard loud shouting as I was heading towards the library. I recognized Scott's voice and another in broken English. Curious, I headed to where the shouts were coming from and saw Scott and the Malaysian guy he shared a cell with screaming in each other's faces.

"Scott, what's going on, mate? Chill out, you're bringing yourself a lot of attention," I said.

"I'm sick of this faggot feeling me up when I'm in bed. He keeps wrapping his legs and arms around me when I'm trying to sleep," screamed Scott into the Malaysian guy's face.

The Malaysian screamed back in badly broken English and then threw the worst punch in the world at Scott's bare chest. Scott reacted by throwing the world's second worst punch into the shoulder of the Malaysian guy. This was hand bags at dawn, I thought, and embarrassing.

"Scott, forget about him. It's not worth getting nicked for. You'll only end up in the Soi," I said, stepping in between the two of them. "Come on, let's go and get a coffee in the library. Leave this for another time," I said and pulled him away from the screaming Malaysian.

Scott followed me to the library and sat down; he was still angry but was slowly calming down. I moved over to the back of the library and began chopping up chillies using Pi Chet's hatchet while Hafiz made us all coffee.

The Malaysian guy had a friend known as Chinese Jimmy, who had a big mouth. He had long, black hair, boy-band looks and fancied himself as a bit of a hard case.

"Hey you, Mr Englishshit, you fight my friend, you fight me," shouted Chinese Jimmy, pointing at Scott who was sitting down and sipping his coffee. My back was turned to the both of them as I continued to chop the chillies for lunch. I turned to see Chinese Jimmy and his Malaysian friend towering over Scott as he sat and drank his coffee. Pi Chet was at his desk, quietly writing in his special "Big Book" – his loan book – and ignoring what was going on in his library. I stopped chopping the chillies, but still had hold of the hatchet.

"Jimmy, leave. We don't want any trouble in here, understand?" I told him calmly. "This is neither my nor your argument," I said.

"Who are you? He my friend. He have problem, I have problem, you piece of English shit," spat Jimmy.

"You want fight me? I will beat your ugly arse," shouted Jimmy as he poked his finger at me. He then spat in my face and laughed.

The only thing separating myself from Chinese Jimmy was a wooden table. The anger surged rapidly inside me. Jimmy must have noticed the evil in my eyes as he slowly backed away from the table with fear in his own. I just saw red. Still with the hatchet in my right hand, I launched myself over the table and charged at Jimmy, raising the hatchet above my head. I wanted to smash this solid piece of sharp metal across his head and rip his skull open like a water melon.

Jimmy ran out the library, followed by his Malaysian friend who was screaming for help. I was close behind him and ready to swing the hatchet deep into his head when Pi Chet managed to stop me.

Blueshirts came running from every direction; I was hit with a sudden clarity and it dawned on me how much trouble I was in when I found myself surrounded by blueshirts. Pi Chet held a lot of respect amongst the trusties and waved them away.

Chinese Jimmy was screaming that he wanted me to be charged for attempting to attack him with the hatchet, but Pi Chet told him to move on and to keep his stupid mouth shut as it was his own fault for making a scene in the library. The blueshirts dispersed, leaving silly Jimmy and his Malaysian friend alone, unwilling to hear their argument about having me sent to the Soi for six months.

I gave Pi Chet his hatchet back, headed back inside the library and sat on the bench next to Mr Lee.

"Mr Billy, may I tell you something?" Mr Lee asked.

"Tell me what you want," I said, not really interested in what he had to say.

"I think it was very bad what you did with Mr Jimmy. You no good man. My feeling about you has changed."

This was rich, coming from a man who had chopped his friend up into eight pieces, so his advice fell on deaf ears.

"OK, Mr Lee, why don't you just carry on and read your Bible," I said.

But I knew that he was right; I could have handled the situation a lot better. If it wasn't for Pi Chet, I would have been in the Soi now, fighting for my arse. Being clean was good, but adding crazy to that was a bad combination. I had to change my behaviour and be more aware of how I reacted to certain situations, or the next time I might not be so lucky.

Job had heard from someone that I was being repatriated and wanted to know if he could transfer back to England with me. I had yet to tell him myself, as I was afraid it would upset him. It was difficult to explain to him that I had to go alone. He told me he had a passport and was convinced he could return with me.

"Glap duay, na," (we go together) he would say constantly. I didn't have the heart to tell him it was impossible. He didn't seem to understand the concept of being locked up. It was really sad to know that I would have to leave him behind, as he had served only three years and would have to remain here for a further thirty-seven.

"Sam sip jet bpee, bpaet duan, chan yiem krap," he would proudly say to anyone who asked what remained of his sentence (thirty-seven years and eight months with excellent class, sir).

His predicament never seemed to bother him, and I was curious to learn more about Job.

His mother was an alcoholic. Sadly, she had had no time for him as a boy, and so he was raised by an aunt. They lived in Lop Buri, a small province north of Bangkok. His father had abandoned him and his mother when she was seven months pregnant with Job. Poor and with no education, a life of crime was all that was available to him.

Job had over 28,000 baht in his private spending account, a small fortune in prison, but still he would eat the government slop that was dished out twice a day, served off a filthy table next to the toilets. I learnt that his aunt would visit him once a week, each time putting money into Job's account. He would also receive a parcel of food from the prison shop – chicken legs, rice, vegetables and a bag of guava fruit – which he would share out amongst his cellmates. I asked why he never purchased items from the canteen. He said he couldn't read or write, and had no idea how to shop.

Before I left for England, I wanted to make sure that Job would be in good condition and eat healthy food. He had already decided he was a Muslim once he saw all the wonderful food we ate at lunch time. Pi Chet had given him a sarong and a skull cap and he would join us each afternoon for Duhar prayer; he was keen and showed willingness. I taught him how to order food from his account; he could spend up to 200 baht a day which was more than enough to survive on. I would order him a meal, usually kao pad gai kai dao – chicken in a hot spicy sauce with rice and a cold fried egg on top – with a piece of lemon for 30 baht; also fruit, whatever was in season for another 30 baht – strawberries, mango, chompu – Thailand had an amazing variety of tropical fruit.

I would add a Thai doughnut that had green slime in the middle, but was tasty, for 15 baht, and finally a vegetable juice drink for another 15 baht. So he only had to spend 90 baht a day and could use whatever remained to buy toiletries. I asked Wang, one of the shopkeepers and a decent fella, to help Job with his shop orders once I was gone; I could trust Wang not to use him like so many others in the prison would.

I was happy with what I had set in place for Job; he would have breakfast each morning in the library, a fried egg on green bread with a mug of hot coffee. At lunch after our prayer, we would all sit down and eat a huge meal, washed down with ice-cold water. Finally, his shop order would be taken back to his cell each evening, therefore making sure he didn't go hungry during the night. I couldn't do anything more for him. I was his buddy and he was my shadow. I was going to miss him.

I had received good news that I was finally to be sent back to the UK within the next couple of weeks. It was now official, and the Thais could not do anything to stop my repatriation. It was mid-March 2010 and there was political unrest in Thailand. The country was on the verge of civil war and I was afraid I would have my transfer delayed. As if that wasn't bad enough, British Airways was on strike at the same time.

On 30 March, the flight I was due to be on was cancelled due to the strike and I was sent back to prison in disbelief. So near and yet so far. Would anything ever go right for me?

Embarrassed, I returned to my cell in a state of paranoid confusion. The next day I was assured the London flight was safe and I would finally be going home.

As the day dawned I said my farewells to my good friends and promised to stay in touch with Scott, who was with me to say goodbye. Rob was now out of the hospital and promised to stay off drugs. He seemed to be back to his normal self.

A huge crowd walked me to the main gate in building six. I felt sad that I was leaving my friends behind in this horrible place that we now called home. We had survived the terrors this dark satanic place had held for each of us because we had looked out for each other. When one of us was weak and failing the rest became collectively stronger and pulled the weak to safety. Our friendships would survive in memories and I knew I would never forget any single one of them.

I emerged through the main gates of building six with extreme relief. When I thought my fellow inmates and now departed friends could no longer see me I allowed myself one last tearful look. I saw them gazing at my shadow as I departed from their lives to my own personal freedom. Each of their now joyful faces masked the individual pain I knew they felt. Would they survive their own hellish prison sentences to make the same journey to freedom? I knew each of them wished that it was them going through those gates and not me. The image of my friends, rooted to the spot, still waving at my shadow, is etched in my mind and will live with me forever.

As the gates closed behind me, two Thai prison guards came forward. Their eyes no longer cold, they knew that from this point they had limited control over me. There was an element of deference in their attitude towards me. I had faced them on their own turf, had survived their hell and torment and in so doing had earned their respect. I started to smile. I was beginning to feel human again.

I was handcuffed to the Thai guards. What little was left of my personal belongings was handed to the guards who also held an envelope containing my release papers and immigration forms. As the prison transport arrived, I was taken to the side door and ushered into the waiting vehicle. Excitement began to well inside me as the van moved forward and the fifteen-minute journey to the airport began.

I did not look back.

At the airport, I was held in the immigration centre for some eight hours, in what seemed like luxury when compared with the satanic surroundings I'd left just fifteen minutes before.

These last eight hours of imprisonment on Thai soil flew past. Time had no meaning. I was going home; nothing else mattered.

The cell doors opened and I heard friendly English voices. Hands outstretched to greet me. Two prison officers from HMP Wandsworth had come to Bangkok to collect me. They removed the Thai handcuffs and replaced them with British ones, explaining that when we were on the plane they would be removed so as not to upset the other passengers.

I didn't care. I was in British custody and going home. Nothing else mattered. The prison officers asked if I was hungry and took me to airport Burger King. A Double Whopper and Fries had never tasted so good. From cold cabbage slop to this; I could have been dining at Buckingham Palace.

On the plane, the officers questioned me endlessly and in detail about my life in a Thai prison, and the long flight passed quickly. I savoured every moment of my new-found luxury. The airplane seat, notoriously uncomfortable in cabin class, was to me the ultimate in comfort and luxury. The aircraft food was warm and welcoming. For the first time in three years I slept the sleep of an angel. I felt safe and secure.

On touchdown at Heathrow I was handcuffed again and escorted to a transit van which was waiting to take me to HMP Wandsworth. This was to be my new home for the next eight months, after which I could finally be free.

Wandsworth prison is considered one of Europe's largest correction centres and holds up to 1,600 inmates. In comparison with the "Bangkok Hilton" it was like a real hotel, but with bars.

I was given three meals a day, had a TV, DVD and CD player, Play Station; I even had my own kettle. But what amazed me even more was that I was in control of something as simple as a light switch.

Because of my injuries, I was placed on the ground floor on A Wing. A1-18 was my cell, the bottom bunk my bed space. It was free and it felt great and I didn't have to buy the bed from a ladyboy!

I had to share my cell with only one other person who took the top bunk. I couldn't believe the whining and moaning from some of the other prisoners in Wandsworth. They would complain about the conditions they lived in and how they were sick of eating chicken every day. It brought a smile to my face to see how ungrateful some people were. I suppose they didn't know any better; this was as bad as it could get for them here in a prison in the UK. They hadn't had to wait in long queues for a bowl of cold cabbage slop or sleep on the floor amongst a mass of stinking bodies, mine being one of them.

I was even given one of the top jobs in the prison, that of gym orderly, so I wasted no time getting myself fit. The responsibility of the job did me good and as each day passed I became stronger mentally and physically. The prison staff at Wandsworth were sympathetic and understanding of my ordeal and I responded in kind to the way they treated me.

I spent almost eight months at HMP Wandsworth before I was released on an amnesty by the King of

Thailand. I immediately moved to Bournemouth in the south of England. I was staying at my friend Jay's flat and sleeping on his sofa. Bournemouth is a beautiful part of the country with a seven-mile long golden-sand beach. I used it as a stepping stone before I moved back to Liverpool to be with my family. My mind was still corrupted with nightmares of all I had had to endure whilst in prison in Thailand and I wanted to be sure that I didn't project this onto my family.

During my time in Bournemouth I kept in touch with my friends in Thailand. I learnt that Scott had been moved to Chiang Rai prison up north and close to the Burmese border to be nearer to Joy. However, Joy was released on an amnesty due to her sentence being six months less than Scott's. Thai law states that an ex-prisoner cannot visit anyone in prison for at least two years so it was really all a waste of time as Joy wasn't allowed to visit Scott. I worried about the effect that this would have on Scott. He was mentally and physically frail when I had left him and any more setbacks might tip him over the edge to drug-obsessed insanity.

Even after his release last year, I still worry whether he will survive. Mitch is now in America, on remand for the drug offence he allegedly committed whilst in Bang Kwang lifers' prison in Bangkok. My good friend Nan received a King's pardon in August 2011 and is now free. Mama and Papa still run the Muay Thai School and boxing teams and we stay in touch. They say they want me to rejoin their community.

Adjusting to life free in the UK has been difficult. I feel emotionally scarred and continue to have nightmares on a regular basis. However, these dreams are becoming less and less frequent. Very few people have endured what I have been through and talking my experiences through with new acquaintances and family friends has proven difficult.

I owe a lot to Donna, the one person who for years never gave up when I have felt the need to unload my thoughts and fears. I have learnt not to do this and now hold onto such emotions, unable to let go. Writing this, my first book, has helped me and, as I reach the conclusion, I am beginning to feel free.

I needed more surgery to repair my hernia and was treated at St George's Hospital in south London. This time I received keyhole surgery, but despite this my hernia reoccurred and still causes me severe pain. A couple of months after my stint at St George's my left leg began to swell and I was taken in considerable pain to the Royal Bournemouth Hospital where a doctor told me that I had numerous blood clots all over my left leg. I was immediately admitted to a ward and spent a month being treated with blood-thinning warfarin tablets. I used my time on the ward to put pen to paper and then used my laptop to commit my memories and feelings to paper. The pain in my left leg was all-consuming and reliving these painful memories and experiences proved too much. Suddenly, I lost all interest and stopped writing, unable to carry on. "Procrastination" springs to mind.

It was time to be with my mother and family and I was ready to move back to Liverpool. My life had been running at a million miles an hour and I just wanted the world to stop. I wanted only to sit down with my mother and family, to rest and recover.

Above all, I just wanted to be me.

Acknowledgements

I WOULD LIKE to thank all the people who helped me get my story down on paper. I am sorry for all the headaches I gave them and I am grateful for their patience.

I would like to thank the charity Prisoners Abroad, because without their help and compassion many British prisoners in foreign jails would suffer more than they do.

The fact that I'm still clean today I owe to the fellowship provided by Narcotics Anonymous.

Finally, although my dad was harsh when we were young, I still love and forgive him for how he behaved when we were kids.